MW00582538

BOYD'S

ℛECITATION
&
DIALOGUE

Plays & Programs
for Special Days of the Year

Published by
The National Baptist Publishing Board
6717 Centennial Blvd., Nashville, Tennessee 37209-1049

BOYD'S

*R*ECITATION & DIALOGUE

Plays & Programs
for Special Days of the Year

Revised 1998

All rights reserved. No part of this publication may be reproduced, stored in a retrieval system, or transmitted in any form or by any means, electronic, mechanical, photocopying, recording, or otherwise, without the prior permission of the copyright owner, except for brief quotations included in review of the book.

Published by
The National Baptist Publishing Board
6717 Centennial Blvd., Nashville, Tennessee 37209-1049

Plans and Programs for Special Days of the Year and Miscellaneous Material including:

THE BIBLE

(Material for Bible Sunday in October;
Children's Bible Bands, etc.)

Blessed Bible! How I Love It

Blessed Bible! How I love it!
How it doth my spirit cheer!
What has earth like this to cover?
O, what stores of wealth are here!
Man was lost and doomed to sorrow,
Not one ray of light or bliss
Could he from earth's treasures borrow,
Till his way was cheered by this.
Yes, I'll to my bosom press thee,
Precious Word, I'll hide thee here;
Sure my very heart will bless thee,
For thou ever say'st "good cheer!"
Speak, poor heart, and tell thy pond'rings,
Tell how far thy rovings led,
When this book bro't back thy wand'rings,
Speak life as from the dead.
Blessed Bible! I will hide thee
Deep, yes, deeper in my heart,
Thou thro' all my life wilt guide me,
And in death we will not part;
Thro' death's vale I'll lean on thee,
Then in words above forever,
Sweeter still thy truths shall be.

– Christian Teacher

BIBLE MEMORY WORK

(What the child learns before he is ten years old will be apt to stay with him all his life. Do not neglect a Bible Memory period every week in your children's meetings.)

Handling The Holy Bible

1. What book is the greatest and best?
   The Holy Bible.

2. Why is the Holy Bible so great and good?
   Because it is God's book.

3. Who should read God's book?
   Everyone who can read.

4. How often should the Bible be read?
   Every day.

5. What does God want?
   God wants the Bible to be an open book for all men, women and children.

6. How many parts are there to the Bible?
   Two parts.

7. What are they named?
   The Old Testament and the New Testament.

8. How many books are there in the Old Testament?
   Thirty-nine.

9. How many books are there in the New Testament?
   Twenty-seven.

10. How many books are there altogether in the Bible?
    Sixty-six.

11. Which is your right hand? Which is your left?

12. When you hold the Bible closed between your hands, which Testament is nearer your left hand?
    The Old Testament.

13. The New Testament is nearer to which hand?
    The right hand.

14. Name the books of the Old Testament.

15. Name the books of the New Testament.

Note for Teachers and Learners: Great care should be taken to repeat the name of each book distinctly, to pronounce correctly, and also to be able to spell each one. In committing to memory it is well to do so by groups as arranged above, repeating from Genesis to Deuteronomy, then a slight pause; and so on through both Testaments.

WHAT MEN HAVE SAID

(From the Gospel Proclaimer)

Matthew Arnold: "To the Bible men will return, and why? Because they cannot do without it."

H.L. Hastings: "Every little while somebody starts up and upsets this Book. And it is just like upsetting a solid cube of granite. It is just as big one way as another, and when you have upset it, it is right side up; and when you overturn it again, it is right side up still."

Henry Clay: "I always have had, and always shall have, a profound regard for Christianity."

John Ruskin: "This book has been the accepted guide of the moral intelligence of Europe for some fifteen hundred years."

Napoleon Bonaparte: "Everything in Christ astonishes me. His spirit overawes me, and His will confounds me. Between Him and whoever else in the world there is no term of comparison. He is truly a being by Himself."

Sir Walter Scott:
> "Within this awful volume lives
> The mystery of mysteries!
> And better had they ne'er been born,
> That read to doubt or read to scorn.

William Cowper:
> "Tis Revelation satisfies all doubts,
> Explains all mysteries, except her own,
> And so illuminates the path of life,
> That fools discover it, and stray no more."

George P. Morris:
> "The mines of earth no treasure give
> That could this volume buy;
> In teaching me the way to live,
> It taught me how to die."

William E. Gladstone: "The biblical order of statements as to the creation may be taken as a demonstrated conclusion and established fact."

John G. Whittier:

> "Here fair lady, is the pearl of price,
> May it prove as such to thee!
> Nay keep thy gold I ask it not,
> For the word of God is free.

Benjamin Franklin: "Young men, my advice to you is that you cultivate and acquaintance with, and a firm belief in the Holy Scriptures; this is your certain interest."

Edmund Burke: "I have read the Bible morning, noon and night, and have ever since been the happier and better man for such reading."

William H. Seward: "The whole hope of human progress is suspended on the ever-growing influence of the Bible."

James A. Garfield: "No man can understand the history of any nation or of the world who does not recognize it in the power of God, and behold his stately going form as he walks among the nations."

Benjamin Harrison: "It is by the influence of Christianity that we shall approach universal peace and adopt arbitration methods of settling disputes."

Abraham Lincoln: "In regard to the Great Book, I have only this to say, that it is the best gift which God has given to man."

George Washington: "It is impossible to rightly govern the world without God and the Bible."

Queen Victoria: "This book is the secret of England's greatness."

John Adams: "The Bible is the best book in the world."

Thomas Jefferson: "Of all the systems of morality, none appears so pure to me, as that of Jesus."

John Quincy Adams: "I have for many years made it a practice to read through the Bible once every year; it is an inexhaustible mine of knowledge and virtue."

Daniel Webster: "If we abide by the principles taught in the Bible our country will go on prospering and to prosper."

Ulysses S. Grant: "Hold fast to the Bible as the sheet anchor of your liberties; write its precepts in your hearts and practice them in your lives."

Andrew Johnson: "I believe in Almighty God, and I believe also in the Bible."

Sir Isaac Newton: "We count the Scriptures to be the most sublime Philosophy. I find more marks of authenticity in the Bible than in any profane history whatever."

James K. Polk: "I have read the sacred Scriptures a great deal, and deeply reverence them as divine truth."

THE BIBLE – OUR BULWARK

The Bible is our bulwark of defense for freedom. When the Bible is read and revered, constitutional government, individual liberty, and the rights of the people are respected. When the Bible is unknown or rejected, despotism, dictatorship or the rule of class hatred prevail. We of America are called to stand for the Bible, for representative government, the Constitution of the United States, the Bill of Rights, for all these high defenses of the good life we seek to cherish. Let us positively, unitedly, loyally uphold the cause we love – the cause for which our fathers came to these shores. Let us firmly maintain the liberty under God to which they dedicated their lives. Let us pass on to our children and our children's children, our rich heritage of Scriptural truth.

– United States Senator James J. Davis

IT IS THE BOOK

All other books have men only as authors; this book is God's Book. It is the most read, the most loved, and the most hated book in the world. Though it is one of the oldest books in the world, it is by far the most modern, anticipating the future, revealing things yet to come. It is the only Book in the world having true prophecies and true types. It reveals a unique plan of salvation, in which the Creator Himself suffered for the sins of His creatures, and then offers eternal life free to all who will accept His Son. It has the only reasonable cosmogony, gives the only true philosophy of life, reveals man and sin as they are, without fear or favor, and gives the only true picture of God to be found anywhere.

– Christian Victory

TEN COMMANDMENTS OF JESUS

First and Greatest Commandment:

Thou shalt love thy Lord thy God with all thy heart, and with all thy soul, and with all thy mind, and with all thy strength. – Mark 12:30.

Second Commandment is like unto it:

Thou shalt love thy neighbour as thyself. – Mark 12:31.

Third, a New Commandment:

Love one another, as I have loved you. – John 13:34.

Fourth, the Hard Commandment:

Love your enemies, bless them that curse you, do good to them that hate you, and pray for them which despitefully use you, and persecute you. – Matthew 5:44.

Fifth, the Golden Commandment:

All things whatsoever ye would that men should do to you, do ye even so to them. – Matthew 7:12.

Sixth, the Shining Commandment:

Let your light so shine before men, that they may see your good works, and glorify your Father which is in heaven. – Matthew 5:16.

Seventh, the Seeking Commandment:

Seek ye first the kingdom of God, and his righteousness. – Matthew 6:33.

Eighth, the Mercy Commandment:

Be ye therefore merciful, as your Father also is merciful. – Luke 6:36.

Ninth, the Highest Commandment:

Be ye therefore perfect, even as your Father which is in heaven is perfect. – Matthew 5:48.

Tenth, the Commission Commandment:

Go ye into all the world, and preach the gospel to every creature. – Mark 16:15.

Conclusion:

If ye love me, keep my commandments. – John 14:15

– Arranged by John L. Wininger

A LIGHT TO MY PATH

– *The Bible* –

"Thy word is a lamp unto my feet, and a light unto my path." Psalm 119:105.

"For ever, O Lord, thy word is settled in heaven." Psalm 119:89.

Other books tell us what man supposes; the Bible tells us what God knows. Other books tell what other men, almost as foolish as ourselves, speculate; this Book tells us what an infinitely wise God, who made us and all things, has inerrantly revealed. This Book makes men wise with the wisdom that is golden, the wisdom that brings eternal salvation. No one can study this Book aright, no matter how ignorant he may otherwise be, without becoming possessed of that priceless wisdom that means eternal life. No other Book has the power to make us acquainted with God and with His Son Jesus Christ, that this Book has. Oh, study the Book that brings eternal life; make it in your own experience, "The implanted word, which is able to save your soul."

"And that from a child thou hast known the holy scriptures, which are able to make thee wise unto salvation through faith which is in Christ Jesus." 2 Timothy 3:15.

"This book of the law shall not depart out of thy mouth; but thou shalt meditate therein day and night, that thou mayest observe to do according to all that is written therein: for then thou shalt make thy way prosperous, and then thou shalt have good success." Joshua 1:8.

"Search the scriptures; for in them ye think ye have eternal life: and they are they which testify of me." John 5:39.

CHILDREN'S DAY

Little Daisies

(Concert Recitation for Girls, each
holding a bouquet of flowers)

We are little daisies
Bursting into bloom,
Blessing by our sweetness
All within the room.

We are tiny rosebuds
Hiding in the green;
Don't we make a nosegay,
Nicest ever seen?

We're our Father's flowers
Planted by his hand;
Will you tend and keep us
For his heavenly land?

The Little Candles

(A Story for Children's Day Services)

Once upon a time, there was a little yellow candle, and a little brown candle, and a little red candle, and a little black candle, and a little white candle, all huddled together in one small box.

You see, it was just after Christmas time, and they were all that was left of the storekeeper's candle supply, so he had taken the red candle, and the yellow candle, and the brown candle, and the black candle, and the white candle out of their own boxes, and there they lay, one on top of the other, all in a jumble.

They had been so proud when they had been alone, touching only their own kind.

"Oh," the red candle said, "I wouldn't touch those brown candles on display next to our box. We are so pretty, but they look so dirty!"

The yellow one had held its head high. "The way those two boxes smell," he had sighed.

And now, there they were, all together! The window where they lay was in broad sunshine most of the day, and as the days went by, the poor little candles got quite hot within their tiny box. They were so hot that they began to melt, and as they began to melt, they began to quarrel.

"Now look here!" cried the little brown candle to the little red candle. "Stop dripping on me! You are spoiling my good looks! Giving me measles, with all those reb blotches of yours!"

"Well," and the little red candle grew redder still with anger, do you think I am any better off? Look at that awful neighbor of mine! He is sprinkling me with freckles, and I certainly am a sight!"

"Don't you think," said the little yellow candle, "that I am suffering more than any of you? That black neighbor of mine makes me look much worse – just as if I had the Black Plague! Oh, if I could only get some air!"

"Oh, if you grumblers would only stop kicking," burst the little black candle. "I am right up against the lid, and every time you kick, I stick to it so that I lose part of my tallow coat. I look as if I had leprosy!"

"What about me?" cried the white candle. "If I'm dripping on you, you're all dripping on me. I am stouter than you are, and you are all touching me! You certainly are a nuisance, you horrid things!"

And they all went on, grumbling and fussing, fuming and kicking, and they still were doing it, when suddenly the cover of the box was forced open, and they heard a voice saying, "Here, ma'am, his will do very well for our party. They are all I have left." Then, in disappointing tones the same voice added, "Well, they are a sight! But I suppose you can scape them off."

"Oh, they'll do just as they are," answered another voice. "I'll take them."

Again the cover was shut, a jerk, a jolt, a tumbling together closer yet, and the little candles were on their way.

A patter of little feet, small children's voices calling out, "Oh good, here are the candles!" and the lid of the box flew open.

"At last, we'll be separated," and the little candles sighed a sigh of relief.

"Oh," a small girl's voice cried, "they are all different!" "How nice! That's just what we wanted." "Here is Jimmy Crow," and out walked the little black candle to take its stand on a high birthday cake. "And here is Ching Lee," a voice proclaimed, and out stepped the little yellow candle. Alas for its pride, it was stuck right next to Jimmy Crow!

"Here goes Sight Arrow," and small fingers stood the little red candle right next to Ching Lee.

The others followed. "Tiny Kim" hopped next to Straight Arrow, "Fat Sammy" was next to him, and now there they stood in a circle on the big birthday cake. And as they all stood together, they saw to their surprise that right in their midst there stood a tall, tall white candle, lighted.

As the little candles stared at the big one, small fingers took them up and, bending their heads, lighted them all at the one big light. As they stood upright again, blinking and winking and nodding, there arose little children's voices saying all together, "Jesus is the Light of the World."

And in the light of the Light of the World, the little yellow, and brown, and red, and black, and white candles looked at each other.

Lo! Each was shining so bright, so bright, that all their spots had disappeared, and all were aglow with Love.

HAPPY SUMMER

Thank God for happy summer,
For green upon the world,
And flowers bright-red, yellow, white –
In the field and lane unfurled;

For wind upon the hilltop
And bird-songs in the boughs,
And clear and high the lovely sky
Arched over every house;

For Sunlight every morning
And beauty everywhere –
Thank God for happy summer time,
The fairest of the year!

– Nancy Byrd Turner

Magic Keys

When I forget and ask for things
Without the magic word,
My mamma keeps on at her work
As if she hasn't heard.

If I say, "Oh, I'm nearly starved,
Give me a piece of bread."
My daddy never bats an eye –
Nor even turns his head

But when I use a "thank you,"
And remember to say "please"–
They open many doors to me,
Just like two magic keys.

Sending Out Smiles

I have some little enemies –
They call themselves "The Blues"
And like all other kind of foes,
They're splendid things to lose.
So when I know they're planning
To come and spend the day,
I send the little smiles out
To chase them all away.

– Exchange

A Boy's Decision

I am a very little boy
But I can fill your heart with joy.
I go to school five times a week
And learn to read and write and speak.

I go to church on Sabbath Day
And listen to what the preachers say.
Then tell me to be nice and kind
To visit the sick and help the blind.

Before I get to be a man
I will also take a stand
And try to be kind and good
And serve my Saviour as I should.

— Mrs. Alberta E. Jordan,
Nashville, TN

Lord of Little Things

Dear Lord of flowers and sparrows
And other little things
That blossom in the grasses,
Or fly about on wings —

You used to watch the birdies,
The butterfly and bee;
And once you took a tiny child
And held him on your knee.

So, then, because I'm little,
I seem to feel you near.
And, if you're wanting little things,
Dear Jesus! See! I'm here!

— Grace H. Patton

Confessing his own lack of understanding of exactly what children want to read, Edwin Francis Edgett, literary editor of the revered Boston Evening Transcript, "can not resist the temptation" to pick out from "Short Poems for Short People," for broadcasting:

15

Be Yourself

It is hard to be a turnip
When you'd like to be a rose.
And 'tis hard to be a cabbage
All the time!

And 'tis also very horrid
Just to be a little boy
When you want to be a monkey,
And to climb!

But, if you're born a boy
Or – a turnip, after all,
It really seems a better
Thing, by far.

To be that boy or turnip,
Just as hard as you can be,
And then, you see, you'll be, just –
What you are.

– Alicia Aspinwall

Recitation

"Like obedient lambs, who follow
Where their shepherd leads each day,
We will follow God, or Leader,
Gladly His commands obey.

With God's goodness all around us,
We no want can every see
When we walk in darkest shadow,
Close beside us He will be.

Goodness, mercy, honor, blessings,
God will give if we are true:
And a home with Him forever
When our journey here is through."

Such As I Have

The little maid sat in a high-backed pew,
And raised to the pulpit her eyes of blue;
The prayers were long, and the sermon grand,
And O, it was hard to understand!
But the beautiful text sank deep in her heart
Which the preacher had made of his sermon a part.
"Silver and gold have I none," said she,
"But such as I have give I to Thee."
And the good old pastor looked down and smiled
At the earnest gaze of the little child.

The dear little maid carried home the word
Determined to use it as chance might afford,
She saw her mother unceasingly
Toil for the needs of the family;
So she cheerily helped the long day through,
And did with here might what her hands found to
    do.
"Silver and gold have I none," said she,
"But such as I have give I to thee."
And the joyful mother tenderly smiled,
As she bent to kiss her little child.

On her way to school at early morn
She plucked blooms by the wayside born.
My teacher is often tired, I know
For we're sometimes naughty and sometimes slow;
Perhaps these may help to lighten her task,
And she laid the flowers on her teacher's desk.
"Silver and gold have I none," said she,
"But such as I have give I to thee."
And the weary teacher looked up and smiled
As she took the gift of the little child.

As she played with her sisters on the grass,
She saw a dusty traveler pass.
"Poor man," said she, "he is tired, I think,

I'll go and get him a nice cool drink."
And she hastened to fetch her little cup,
And dip the sparkling nectar up.
"Silver and gold have I none" said she
"But such as I have give I to thee."
And the thirsty, dusty traveler smiled
As he took the cup from the little child.

Sweet and innocent, clad in white,
She knelt by her little bed at night,
With a childish trust she longed to bring
Some gift to her Saviour and her King.
"So much from Thee every day I receive,
But my heart is all that I have to give.
"Silver and gold have I none," said she,
"But such as I have give I to thee"
And our Father looked down and tenderly smiled
As He took the gift of the little child.

Bible Children

(By using the following references you can give each of the children who can read the Bible well, a place on your Children's Day Program. If you do not wish to use all of the references, due to lack of time on the program, choose the references you think will be of greatest interest and helpfulness to the children.)

A righteous child – Abel. Genesis 4:4; Matthew 23:35

An unrighteous child – Cain. Genesis 4:3, 8

A disobedient child – Phinehas. 1 Samuel 2:12-17, 34.

An obedient child – Samuel. 1 Samuel 3:1-10

A vain child – Absalom. 2 Samuel 1:25, 26; 18:9

A devoted child – Joseph. Genesis 30:24; 47:11

A worldly child – Esau. Genesis 25:32-34

A covetous child – Jacob. Genesis 25:31-34

A lame child – Mephibosheth. 2 Samuel 4;4; 9:3-10

A *strong child* – Samson. Judges 13:24; 14:6; 15:16

A *hidden child* – Joash. 2 Kings 11:2, 3

A *saved child* – Moses. Exodus 2:1-10

A *faithful child* – Jonathan. 1 Samuel 31:1, 2

A *fortunate child* – Benjamin. Genesis 35:18

A *promised child* – Isaac. Genesis 17:16

A *wise child* – Solomon. 1 Kings 3:5-14

A *beloved child* – David. 1 Samuel 16:12; 1 Chronicles 2:15

A *devout child* – Timothy. 2 Timothy 1:5; Acts 16:1, 2

A *perfect child* – Jesus. Luke 2:52

We Are Daisies

(Five or six primary children troupe on the stage singing the following song to the tune of "When He Cometh, to Gather His Jewels." The children are dressed in yellow and white cambric or cheesecloth and carry armsful of white field daisies.)

We are daisies, growing daisies
Abloom in life's garden.
Ever growing, ever showing
Our faces so bright.
We are growing for Jesus
To brighten His kingdom,
See we lift up our faces
To bask in the light.

We are daisies, nodding daisies
Soft winds sweeping o'er us,
But we're stronger, ever stronger
If rooted in love.
So we're giving for Jesus
Our lives unto others,
'Til he gathers us into
His garden above.

CHRISTMAS MATERIAL
Boundary of Christmas

Christmas is bounded on the north by Happiness, Good Wishes, Oyster Lake, and the isthmus of Cranberry Sauce; on the east by the peninsula of Turkey and Ocean of Goodies; on the south by Mince Pie, Jellies and Cakes, on the west by Pleasant Words, from which it is separated by the mountains of cheerfulness. The capitals of Christmas are Peace and Good Will, on the Christmas Tree River.

Dear teachers, friends and schoolmates, we are now on the border of this happy country, and before entering we wish you all a "Merry Christmas and a Happy New Year."

Welcome

(For Christmas Service)
Welcome, welcome! Merry Christmas!
Just hear the sounds of glee!
Welcome, welcome! Merry Christmas!
Welcome to our Christmas Tree.

Grandma's Mistake

(For a very little girl)
Poor Grandma! I do hate to tell her!
And yet it does seem very queer,
She's lived so much longer than I have,
And I – why, I've known it a year!
Even Alice begins to look doubtful,
And she is so babyish, too,
And Mamma slyly laughs at the nonsense,
But Grandma believes it is true!

I did it all up in brown paper,
And laid it just there by her plate;
She put on her glasses so slowly,
I thought that I never could wait.
But when she had opened the bundle,
"My gracious!" she said, "how complete!"

A dear little box for my knitting –
Now isn't old Santa Claus sweet?

"To think that the funny old fellow
Should notice I needed just this!
If he should come in here this morning,
I think I should give him a kiss!"
She never once looked at me, never;
Of course, I had nothing to say
But I was so mortified, truly,
I just had to run right away.

Poor Grandma! I do hate to tell her!
But some day, of course, she'll find out,
And then she will laugh to remember
What once she was puzzled about.
But as for that beautiful work-box,
She laid with such care on the shelf,
How can she think Santa Claus brought it?
I made the thing for her myself!

The Quest of the Magi

A Dramatization of Matthew 2:1-12

CHARACTERS: Balthasar, Melchior, Gaspar, Herod, Nathan, Elias, Josiah, Courtiers, Mary, Joseph, The Magi, Scribes

Scene I

Concealed reader gives Matthew 2:1, 2. Three men in rich Oriental garb pass slowly before curtain while singer off platform gives a solo, "There Came Three Kings at Break of Day" (Abingdon Hymnal), or "We Three Kings of Orient Are" (Hymnal for American Youth). Each man carries tall, ornamented staff. Eyes raised to strong light above and off platform. Tinkle of camel bells heard from a distance. For this scene the auditorium should be dark, all light seeming to come from the star that leads the Magi.

21

Scene II

Curtains are drawn, disclosing the court of Herod the Great in Jerusalem. Herod seated in carved chair on raised dais covered with Oriental rug. He wears the purple robe of royalty, fashioned after the Roman manner, with a gold band around his forehead, confining his black hair. Courtiers in colorful costumes are grouped on either side of the throne. Herod is in a dark mood, and drums nervously with fingers on arm of chair. Courtiers watch him furtively, secretly fearful, outwardly smiling. Soft music of harp or string ensemble heard off platform. Page enters, bows low, and stands with arms folded across breast, waiting permission to speak. Herod glowers at him a moment in silence. Then . . .

HEROD: Art thou dumb? Speak, before I have thy tongue torn out.

PAGE (bowing): My lord, the men of whom thou hadst word yesterday are asking strange questions of all they meet, and there is much tumult in the city.

HEROD: Impudent meddlers! But that they seem persons of distinction I would soon put them where they would ask not more questions! (mocking) "Where is he that is born King of the Jews?" I am king of the Jews, by the will of Caesar and the power of my own purpose! They have no other king, nor ever shall have. I swear it! The more it galls them to see an Idumean on the thrown of David, the more it pleases me. This child's prattle of a star that led men from the East – laugh at it!

COURTIER: (bowing obsequiously): It is, of a truth, but witless babble, fit only to make sport for Herod and his friends. Ha, ha! (courtiers join in laughter)

HEROD: Silence, fools! (laughter is instantly hushed) I fear no earthly rival for my throne, but in the sacred writings it is said that there shall come One – (falls into brooding silence, which none dare break) "Born – King of the Jews." (pauses) That might mean that he is of the

22

line of David. If there were such a one all Jewry would
– (pauses, then to page) Ha, dullard! Bring to me
scribes who know what Hebrew prophets have to say
about this One who is to come – and let thy feet be
nimbler than thy tongue.

PAGE (bowing): I go, my lord king. Music grows louder, "Hail
to the brightness of Zion's Glad Morning" lends itself
well to this scene. Much emphasis on closing strains.
Courtiers watch Herod, as before. At final triumphant
chord of the music.

HEROD (fiercely): Silence that noise! By all the gods, I'll
send to the gallows those twangers of harpstrings!
Give me the roll of drums, the clang of cymbals, the
blare of trumpets – anything but the ceaseless wail of
harps and violas. (courtier hurries off; music ceases)
How much longer am I to wait for those gray-beards?

2nd COURTIER: I think I hear them approaching, O king.

HEROD: Keep thy thoughts to fill thy empty head. Have I not
ears as well as thou?

(Enter page, breathless, followed by scribes; richly
dressed and dignified men with long white beards; heads
covered with drapery. (See Bible for details.) The first carries reverently a large parchment "book" – light brown paper
rolled on two wooden rods having folded ends. They salute
Herod with cold courtesy; he stares at them insolently.)

HEROD: And who are ye?

NATHAN: Nathan ben Azariah, O king. (bows)

ELIAS: Elias ben Zadok, O king. (bows)

JOSIAH: Josiah ben Levi, O king. (bows)

HEROD: What have ye there? (points to roll)

NATHAN: The book of the prophet Micah, O king.

HEROD (leaning forward, and looking fixedly at Nathan): It
is said that there are strangers in the city who ask
questions about One who is born King of the Jews.
Doth the prophet speak of such a person?

NATHAN (gravely): He does, O king. Wilt thou hear his
words?

As Herod nods, Elias and Joshua step to either side of Nathan. Each takes one of the wooden rods, moving off a little distance so that the parchment is open before Nathan, in center. He reads Matthew 2:6 slowly and distinctly, following text with finger. A long pause. Herod in deep thought. Then, abruptly . . . .)

HEROD: It is enough. Go back to the Temple, O scribes, and pore over your parchments. Now let the strangers be brought before me without delay.

PAGE (bowing): Even now they are in waiting, O king. (As scribes exit, the Magi enters and salute Herod, who smiles and greets them with the utmost graciousness.)

HEROD: Welcome to our court, O venerable sages from the East. We have heard of your quest, and have called ye into our presence to offer such help as may prosper it. But first we would hear what led ye to undertake a journey so long and full of hardship.

BALTHASAR: O king, in the East thy servants spent much time in contemplation of the heavens. One night a strange new star appeared, marvelous for size and brilliancy. It hung just above the horizon and seemed to beckon us. We knew the portent – that a King was born. With one accord we made ready our camels and followed the star, which led us to this city. But now we see it not, and must seek other guidance if we are to find him who is born King of the Jews.

HEROD: At what time, O wise ones, did the star appear?

(Balthasar, Gaspar and Melchior confer. It is evident that they do not agree. One nods, another shakes his head. At last . . . .)

BALTHASAR: That we cannot say with exactness, O king. We have been long on the way, and so closely have we watched that glorious star that we have taken no account of the movements of the others heavenly bodies. It is weeks since first we saw the star; a month; perhaps more.

24

HEROD (lightly, after a moment's thought): But if ye find the infant King, what matters it? Go now to Bethlehem, the city of David, for there the prophets say that Christ should be born. Go and search diligently for the young Child, and when ye have found him bring me word again, that I may come and worship him also.

(Herod smiles and gives a courteous gesture of dismissal. The Magi bow and exit, slowly and with dignity. As Herod looks after them his smile changes to a frown and he drops his chin into the palm of one hand, staring straight ahead with narrowed eyes while he plans the slaughter of the innocent. – Curtain.)

Scene III

(Same as Scene I, except that instead of a staff, one of the Magi carries a gold crown on a crimson cushion; another a silver censer swung from slender chains, and the third a crystal container of myrrh (some dark substance). Their faces show great gladness that they are again led by the star. Reader off platform gives Matthew 2:9, 10. Song, also off platform, "Star of the East," or, "O Little Town of Bethlehem."

Scene IV

(Curtain is drawn to show Mary standing in doorway of "the house," one or two steps above floor of platform. She wears long blue robe over white gown. Head covered by flowing white veil. In her arms she holds the wrapped figure of the child, nothing of face or form being shown. Beside her, on platform, stands Joseph, his eyes fixed on Mary. See Hofmann's picture, "Worship of the Magi" for detail (Wilde's Bible Pictures. No. 20).

JOSEPH: Why is thy gentle smile so deep, Mary, Mary?

MARY: It is the secret I must keep, Joseph, Joseph – The joy that will not let me sleep, the glory of the coming days, when all the world shall turn to praise God's goodness, Joseph . . . .

JOSEPH: What is the message come to thee, Mary, Mary?

MARY: I hear, like wind within the tree, Joseph, Joseph, or like a far-off melody, His deathless voice proclaiming peace, and bidding ruthless wrong to cease, Joseph, Joseph.

(– Bliss Carmen)

(Mary ceases speaking and tenderly adjusts wrapping of the Child. The Magi enter and bow low, repeating in unison, "Hail, thou that art highly favored, the Lord is with thee. Blessed art thou among women . . . Thou hast found favor with God." Mary smiles, and holds Child closer to her breast. Balthasar advances with crown and kneels.)

BALTHASAR: O child of wonder, born King of the Jews and of the hearts of men, behold the golden crown which is the earthly symbol of thy royalty. Led by thy natal star we have journeyed from distant lands to adore thee and pledge ourselves as thy loyal subjects. (Places crown at Mary's feet.)

GASPAR (kneels beside Balthasar): O Child of wonder, born King of the Jews and of the hearts of men, frankincense do I offer thee in token of thy Deity. Thou shalt be great, and shalt be called the Son of the Highest; and the Lord God shall give unto thee the throne of thy father David. (Places censer beside crown.)

MELCHIOR (kneels beside Gaspar): O Child of wonder, born King of the Jews and of the hearts of men, I bring thee myrrh which speaks of thy mortality. Thou art both Son of God and Son of man, and thou must die. But, dying, thou shalt bring life and immortality to light. (places myrrh with other gifts.)

MARY (with gentle dignity): Sirs, in my Son's name I thank thee. (slowly, and with soft musical accompaniment) My soul doth magnify the Lord, and my spirit hath rejoiced in God my Saviour. He hath regarded the low estate of his handmaiden: for, behold, from henceforth all generations shall call me blessed. He that is mighty hath done to me great things; and holy is his name. His mercy is on them that fear him from generation to generation.

(Mary turns slowly and enters the house. Joseph follows, bearing the gifts. Music ceases. The Magi rise and confer together as reader off platform gives Matthew 2:12. Camel bells heard outside. The three turn toward house, raise hands in gesture of benediction, and exit slowly. Burst of triumphant music – "Joy to the World," or the Hallelujah Chorus.)

Christmas Giving

We've packed a box with Christmas toys
    That came to us last year;
Not broken dolls and worn-out books,
    But treasures we hold dear.

For Mother says that gifts we give
    At Christmas time, should not be
Cast off things, but gifts of love,
    The best we have, you see.

And so we plan to send this box
    To little girls and boys,
Who won't have much on Christmas Day,
    Unless we share our toys.

Glad Tidings

Surely this strife-ridden world will pause awhile at Christmas. If it does, it will be an immeasurable tribute to its only universal Saviour. What if it is but a brief interlude in the drama of war, it is also a prophecy of a future peace.

To Dyonisius the Little, a Scythian by birth and an abbot at Rome, A.D. 526, we are indebted for our present chronology. He placed the birth of Christ in the 754th year of Rome.

Since then, this date has been the starting point of our reckoning. Every man, whether Christian or infidel, who dates a letter or ledger is bearing some testimony or doing some honor to Jesus Christ. The coming year ought to be 1967 or 1968 instead of 1964; of that there is now no doubt. We know that Christ was born before the death of Herod the Great, and it is now agreed that his death took place in the month of April, in the 750th year of Rome. Nevertheless, it was a grand conception of Dynoisius to date our era from the birth of our Lord.

The whole air at the first Christmastide was tremulous with joy. It was a time for holy song, for inspired paean, for seraphic praise. If only the world had not obstructed God's mercy and grace so completely, the rhapsodies which range above the Judean hills would be ringing in the hearts of men everywhere today. And yet, in spite of bitter opposition and cunning expediency which aims to keep Christ out of human hearts, he has won his way into the darkest places on this earth. No one can defeat Him. He counts His victories by the lives He saves. These are the vanguard of a new and better day.

Let joy come still to our homes and hearts. Remove whatever obstructs. "Lift up your heads, for your redemption draweth nigh." Christ ever gives brightness and beauty, gladness and glory to the whole circle of life and duty.

But Christ must be born in each heart in order that we may have a true Christmas. Are we rejoicing in the gifts of human love? Shall we be unmindful of Him who is the "unspeakable gift?" Turn not Christ away from the heart's inn; banish Him not to some outside manger. Heaven's gift is now offered without money and without price. Let us say to Him: "Come, Lord Jesus, there shall be room for thee in the stable; now our best is thine. Only honor us with thy beneficent presence."

Christ came to give peace, and from heaven's throne today He gives peace to all who trust Him.

The Star

Over the legends and myths of the ages,
Ghostly and vague as the most of them are,
Shedding Love's light over history's pages,
Shines in bright splendor the blest Christmas star.

Brightly it beamed over Bethlehem's slumber,
Guiding the Wise Men to where Jesus lay;
Blessed joy bringing to souls beyond number
Down through the ages, on each Christmas Day.

Shine in our hearts, blessed star of redeeming,
Guide us to Jesus the world's Saviour-king;
GIve us a life beyond surface and seeming,
Make our hearts worthy his praises to sing.

For Everybody

That night, when in Judean skies the mystic star dispensed
its light

A blind man moved in his sleep and dreamed that he had
sight.

That night when shepherds heard the song of hosts angelic
choiring near,

A deaf man stirred in slumber's spell – and dreamed that he
could hear.

That night when in the cattle stall a mother her child did
hold

A cripple turned his twisted limbs and dreamed that he was
whole.

That night when o'er the newborn babe, the tender Mary
rose to lean,

A loathsome leper smiled in sleep and dreamed that he was
clean.

That night when to the mother's breast the little King was
held secure

A harlot slept a happy sleep and dreamed that she was pure.

That night when in the manger lay the sanctified who came
   to save
A man moved in the sleep of death and dreamed there was
   no grave.

The Birthday of the Holy Christ

This is the Birthday of the Holy Christ –
The Christmas season, set apart to Him
And grateful thoughts of Heaven's great Gift to
   earth,
The lowly manger where a Babe He lay
Has come to be the altar of our hope;
The cross-tree, where He died for sinful men,
Has come to be a gift-tree for the world.
This is the day when happy children sing
And keep with praise the Birthday of the King.
And fitly, too; for children long ago
Sang praises to Him in the temple court,
And made his heavy spirit glad again.
Dear Christ, they must be dull of heart and ear
      who feel no answering thrill of gratitude
When little children sing in praise of Thee!

The Story

Three camels came long ago
   With gilded trappings all aglow
And bearing Wise Men from afar
   Led by a bright and shining star
To where a precious Baby lay
   On that first far-off Christmas Day.
They brought Him gifts from everywhere –
   Pure gold, frankincense and myrrh.
They worshiped Him, the Son of Glory,
   Then went away to tell the Story.
'Tis now my treasure, sweet, sublime,
   Gift of yesterdays, echoes of time.

I am not wise like those of old,
  I have no gifts of shining gold.
Nor frankincense and myrrh to give –
  I have only a little life to live;
Lord, I give You that and all it yields
  Of hearts and souls and harvest fields
To keep the Story young always –
  I give You these this Christmas Day.

– R.D.B.

Christmas Bells

(Exercise for one speaker and two singer – Primary)
(Sound of bells in the distance)

Speaker: Why do bells for Christmas ring?
        Why do little children sing?

Song: (Duet sung to the tune of "Jesus Love Me," only the
      verse I used – no chorus.)

> Once a lovely shining star
> Seen by wise men from afar
> Gently moved until its light
> Made a manger cradle bright.
>
> There a darling baby lay,
> Pillowed soft upon the hay;
> And its mother sang and smiled,
> "This is Christ, the Holy Child."

Speaker: Therefore bells for Christmas ring.
        Therefore little children sing.

"Chris'mus Is A - Comin'"

> Bones a-gittin' achy,
> Back a-feelin' col';
> Han's a growing shaky,
> Jes' lak I was ol',
> Fros' erpon de meddah'
> Lookin' mighty white;
> Snowdraps lak a feddah
> Slippin' down at night.
> Jas' keep t'ings, a-hummin'

Spite O' fros' an' showahs,
Chris'mus is a-comin'
An all de week is ouahs.
Little mas' ai-axin'
"Who is Santa Claus?"
Meks it kin' O' taxin'
Not to brek de laws.
Chillan's pow'ful tryin
To a pusson's grace
W'en dye go a-pryin'
Right on th'oo you' face
Down ermong yo' feelin's;
Jes' pears lak dat you
Got change you' dealin's
So's to tell 'em true.
An' my pickaninny –
Dreamin' in his sleep!
Come hyeah, Mammy Jinny,
Come an'tex a peep.
Ol' Mas' Bob an' Missis
In dye house up daih
Git on chile 'lak dis is.
D'ain't npne anywhaih.
Sleep my little lammy,
Sleep, you little lamb,
He don' know whut mammy
Done save up fu' him.
Dey'll be banjo pickin'
Dancin' all night the'oo.
Dey'll be lots o'chicken,
Plenty tu'ky, too.
Drams to wet you' whistles
So's to drive out chills.
Whut I keer fu' drizzles
Fallin' on de hills?
Jes' keep t'ings a-hummin'
Spite o'col' an' showahs,
Chris'mus day's a-comin,'
An' all de week is ouahs.

– Paul Lawrence Dunbar

A Christmas Sonnet

How far we seem from that calm, holy night
On which the Lord came down to dwell on earth.
How dimly shines for us that radiant light
Which led the wise men to his place on birth.
Our hearts are full, as was the inn of old;
With tinsel glitter are our spits bound;
Upon our ears rings not the song retold,
Our earth-bound thoughts drive out celestial
     sound.

Oh, star! That shone above the quiet inn,
Send down y our light across the ages gone,
Shine through the blackness of indifferent sin,
Enter our hearts which have been closed so long.
Grant to us now the calm, the peace, the love
Thou gavest that night – thy gift form Heaven
     above.

A Song and A Star

Down through the ages,
Of seeking and striving,
Of suffering and misery,
Of grief and despair, –
Star-gleams and song-echoes
Piercing the darkness,
The noise and confusion
Men make in the world.
Contentedly sleeping,
On hillsides at midnight,
The flocks of all ages
Are watched by wise-fools,
Wide awake in the silence
And deep peace of Nature,
Listening and hearing,
Feeling and seeing,
Arising and following
A song and a star.

Recitation

In Bethlehem, one star-lit night,
A beautiful babe was born;
A child whose life was to bless mankind
From that first Christmas morn.

He was not born in a palace grand,
But his was a manger bed;
Turned away from the inn, they went to the
    stalls
Where the loving kind were fed.

They had come to the town along with the
    crowd,
Their taxes there to pay;
But the town knew not, in its worldly ways.
The joy of the coming day.

But the shepherds watched their flock by
    night,
A great white star beheld;
And a wonderful song from the heavenly
    choir,
Sweeter and clearer welled.

A Tree of Stars

Christmas decorations in the church are silent contributions to the success of the entire Christmas program. Don't cut them out of your plans this year because they are "too expensive." At least plan to have a tree, if possible, which can be very effective and inexpensively original. Have you ever trimmed the Christmas tree with gold and silver stars? The children may make five pointed stars of gold and silver papers, doubling the stars and pasting a long loop of green cord between the two sides. The smaller stars are to be hung upon the tree before the Sunday school assembles, the larger stars, six of them, to be hung upon the tree by six primary or junior children, as they repeat the following passages of

Scripture from memory. It will be noted that these are all "Star" references.

First Child – Psalm 90:1, 2. Before the stars were made.

Second Child – Genesis 1:16-18. The story of the time when the stars first appeared in the heavens.

Third Child – Psalm 19:1, 2. The heavens tell of God's power.

Fourth Child – Psalm 147:4. The heavenly Father knows all the stars by name.

Fifth Child – Psalm 8:3-9. God's children are more to Him then all the stars that shine.

Sixth Child – Matthew 2:1-11. The star that guided the Wise Men to the Christ Child.

If electric lights are procurable, strings of them will make the stars shine very realistically. A strong light focused from above on the tree will also add to the glistening of the stars, "We Three Kings of Orient Are" may be sung by the entire school at the close of this exercise.

To Christmas Town

(A playlet for several primary of junior children. The children troupe in and greet each other gayly.)

First Child: Where are you going?

Second Child: We're trying to find Christmas Town.

First Child: So are we. Strange, that it should be hard to find. O here's a gate. "Unselfish," it is marked. That ought to be the road. O dear, it's locked.

Second Child: Here's another gate. But it can't be the way.

(Several say: "Surely not." "No, no," and so forth.)

Second Child: But it's unlocked. Let's try it.

(Several pull the child back as she starts through with exclamations of disapproval.)

Third Child: "Selfish" Gate will never lead to Christmas Town. Perhaps we can find the key to the other gate.

Fairy: (entering from side stage in long flowing white robe with shining head piece and wand) – I will help you find the keys.

First Child: Oh will you please give us the key? See. There are three padlocks.

Fairy: That I have the keys is true, But I cannot give them to you. Till you tell me what they are.

First Child: You mean we are to guess?

Fairy: Not guess, but think. For unless with heart and mind, the Christmas secret you shall find. You cannot use the keys.

Second Child: Oh, I know, one must be LOVE.

Fairy: You've found one key. (Gives it to child)

Third Child: And one, I'm sure is SERVICE. We are getting to be big children now. We should think of doing things for others at Christmas time more than of having things done for us.

Fairy: You've found a second key. (Gives it to child)

First Child: I wonder . . . Could the third be WORSHIP? Sometimes we get to thinking of Christmas as just a time to get and give presents, and to have a big dinner and lots of candy and nuts. We forget the Christ child who made Christmas possible.

Fairy: And the third key goes to you. Open and pass gayly through. Christmas town's not hard to find. If sought with loving heart and mind. With service kind and worship true. Goodbye. A Merry Christmas to you!

(Fairy backs off stage. The children open the gate and pass through singing, "It Came Upon a Midnight Clear." Some other carol may be used if it is more familiar.)

My Christmas Gift

I shall have gifts at Christmas
And shall I fail to bring

My Christmas gift – a loving heart –
To Jesus Christ the King?

I shall sing songs at Christmas –
Let every song I sing
Give honor to the Saviour,
To Jesus Christ the King.

I shall greet friends at Christmas;
Let me not fail to pray,
And greet the King of Christmas
On His glad Christmas day.
— (Author Unknown)

EASTER OR RESURRECTION SUNDAY
EASTER ACROSTIC

Immortality

An acrostic for eleven children. Each child bearing a letter made of cardboard covered with silver payer. The letters bearing the word, "Immortality."

I am the resurrection, and the life; he that believeth in me, though he were dead, yet shall he live.

M y kingdom is not of this world; if my kingdom were of this world, then would my servants fight, that I should not be delivered to the Jews; but now is my kingdom not from hence.

M y soul is exceeding sorrowful, even unto death; tarry ye here, and watch with me.

O ught not Christ to have suffered these things, and to enter into his glory?

R ise, let us be going; behold, he is at hand that doth betray me.

T he Son of man must suffer many things, and be rejected of the elders and chief priests and scribes, and be slain and be raised the third day.

37

A nd they shall scourge Him and put Him to death.

L et these sayings sink down into you ears; for the Son of man shall be delivered into the hands of men.

I t is enough.

T hus it is written and thus it behooved Christ to suffer, and to rise from the dead the third day.

Y et a little while, and the world seeth me no more; but ye see me; because I live, ye shall live also.

Bird and Flower Voices

(For Primary Children)

1. I heard a bird sing Easter Day –
   And this is what he seemed to say –

2. This refrain may be spoken, or sung to the tune of the refrain "Rejoice, Ye Pure in Heart".
   Fear not, fear not, fear not; for God is love.

3. For God, who made them, knows their needs.
   And daily all the birds He feeds.

2. Fear not, fear not, fear not, for God is love.

4. And God, who feeds the birds, will care
   For all His children everywhere.

2. Fear not, fear not, fear not, for God is love.

5. Christ says, though flowers speak not, they too
   Bring us the same sweet message true.

2. Fear not, fear not, fear not; for God is love.

6. For God is beauty clothes each flower,
   He sends the needed sun and shower.

2. Fear not, fear not, fear not; for God is love.

7. And God, who clothes the flowers, will care
   For all His children everywhere.

2. Fear not, fear not, fear not; for God is love.

If Easter Be Not True

If Easter be not true,
    Then all the lilies low must die;
    The Flanders poppies fade and die;
    The spring must lose her fairest bloom,
    For Christ were still within the tomb –
If Easter be not true.

If Easter be not true,
    Then faith must mount on broken wings;
    Then hope no more immortal spring;
    Then hope must lose her mighty urge,
    Life prove a phantom, death a dirge –
If Easter be not true.

If Easter be not true,
    'Twere foolishness the cross to bear,
    He died in vain who suffered there;
    What matter though we laugh or cry,
    Be good or evil, live or die –
If Easter be not true?

If Easter be not true –
    But it is true, and Christ is risen!
    And mortal spirit from its prison
    Of sin and death with Him may rise!
    Worthwhile the struggle, sure the prize,
Since Easter, aye, is true!

                    – Harry H. Barstow

The Hands of Christ

Christ's hands were held in rapture sweet
    Against His mother's breast;
Once they worked with a will we're told,
    And at night were folded in rest.
Once they were laid in healing force
    On the sick, the blind and the lame;
Once they stretched forth in firm command

And the dead from the dark grave came.
Once they rested in blessing sweet,
 On the heads of the children, wee;
Once they were raised in defiance bold,
 And caused publicans to flee.
Once they were stretched on the cross, we know.
 And nailed there for all to see;
Once they opened the door of the tomb,
 To bring eternal life to me.
Today they are reaching tenderly
 Out to a world of sin;
Today they are beckoning to you and me
 To guide us back to Him.
Reach out and clasp those guiding hands,
 They were nailed to the cross for you;
They'll lift you and ease you and carry you on.
 To Him when your journey is through.

The First Easter

They who loved Him and they who hated
 Have stood together beside His cross,
And these are resting in wicked triumph,
 And those are mourning their bitter loss;
How they had hoped He should yet redeem them,
 Had owned Him Master and known Him
 Friend –
Oh, Star of Jacob; too early setting,
 By clouds o'ershadowed, is this the end?
Soldiers and people and priests and rulers
 Wreaked their malice and angry spite,
Though invisible angel legions
 Only waited His word to smite;
Saviour of men and strong Deliverer,
 Himself he would not, could not save,

And cruel hands have seized and slain Him
  And set their seal on His guarded grave.
Giver of life, to death a hostage,
  Lord of glory, in shame who died,
King of kings, by His foes defeated,
  Mocked and beaten and crucified,
Light of the world, in darkness lying,
  Maker of earth, in bondage held –
Surely, Israel's hope has perished,
  Surely, the doom of good is kneeled.
Cometh the dawn of the Easter morning,
  Cometh the flashing of angel wings;
Oh, ye timorous hearts despairing!
  Myrrh and aloes are needless things,
He who was dead is risen – risen!
  His words or comfort your gift shall dim;
And out of the grave of our sins and sorrows –
  We who love Him – we rise with Him.

Resurrection

The word was in the sunbeams,
They wrote it on the blue
Which spread that Easter Sunday
Above my ruptured view,
The word was "Resurrection,"
An Easter message, write
In fair illumination,
Where all might look on it.

One word the birds were singing,
The blackbird, thrush, and lark;
One message, sweetly winging,
While still the hours were dark.
That word was "Resurrection;"

I heard the cheery song,
In garden, field, and woodland,
From all the feathered throng.

A little bee came humming
Along the wood that day,
And around my shoulders booming,
He sand the same sweet lay.
He told of "Resurrection,"
Awakened from the sleep
Of winter, he that morning,
His Easter day would keep.

And then the church bells chiming,
Rang out the same sweet tale,
That told of "Resurrection,"
And life beyond death's vale.
We sang of it that morning;
The pastor preached it, too;
And from the Holy Volume
We proved the glad news true.

A Daily Calvary

We like to think of Calvary
As being far away,
And cast on others all the blame
Of crucifixion day.

True, our hands did not wield the scourge,
Nor nail Him to the tree,
Nor thrust the spear into His side
That day on Calvary.

But our sins wound the loving Christ}
And place Him on the tree;
Our words of scorn still pierce His side –
A daily Calvary.

At The Crucifixion

With taunts and jeers they lifted Him on high,
And with a thud His cross fell to its place;
They scorned the anguish in His wondrous face
And watched Him there, gloating that he must die.

42

His soul in loving grief did deeply sigh
>For those in ignorance who spurned His grace;
>Who cared not that His love should them embrace,
Nor thought they would to Him for mercy cry.

Thousands today put Him to open shame,
>They spurn as naught His majesty, nor deign
>To pause to pray the last respect to Him.
Each knee shall bow before His peerless name,
>The souls that scorned shall cry for grace in vain;
>But those that loved shall wear love's diadem.

Let's Plant Some Trees Today

First – Let us plant a tree of Faith, where all
>Who pass this way may see;
Second – And down beside the gray stone wall
>We'll plant another tree,
>And it shall bear the name of Love,
>And all its fruit will golden be;
First – And then we'll plant two evergreens,
>One for you and one for me;
>And both of them we'll label Truth;
>And Hope must stand right here,
>To keep the others company,
>And banish needless fear;
Second – And Charity must be good soil,
>With lots of room to grow;
>And all about its noble roots
>A crop of kindness we will sow.
Both– And if we keep the ground well tilled,
>And cultivate with love,
>We'll have a place somewhat akin
>To heaven up above.

– Harriet Markham Gill

Spring Time

"Hurry!" says spring,
To the sleeping flowers.
"Time to wake up!"
Say the sunshine and showers.
"Hurry!" says spring,
To the birds a-wing.
"Time to build nests!"
Hear the south wind sing.

"Hurry!" says spring,
To each sleeping thing,
All things wake up,
And are glad it is spring.

– Laura Emily Mau

The Resurrection Day

All hail the Resurrection Day,
    When Christ the Victor rose,
And from the tomb again came forth
    Triumphant o'ere His foes.
Nor stone nor seal nor Roman power
    Could hold the Lord of Life;
He spoke the word and the arose
    A Victor in the strife.
Let men unite the praise His name
    And magnify His love;
So worthy is He of our praise
    All other names above.
Ye ransomed saints, behold your King,
    Who bore your load of sin,
And opened wide the gates of heaven
    That you might enter in.
All hail the Resurrection Day!
    All hail our glorious King!
The Lamb of God has conquered death,
    While saints his praises sing.

Victory Over Death

With sun eclipsed and earthquake shock,
  The crucifiers fled;
And pain-stricken spread the word,
  "The Christ! The Christ – is dead!"

The fate of Jesus on the cross,
  Brought night and dark despair;
Man's faith in him seemed turned to dust,
  And vain the voice of prayer.

Death sealed the tomb with tears and grief,
  When friends laid Christ a way;
Earth's hopes were crushed and all seemed lost,
  Upon that dismal day.

Another day was yet to dawn,
  The day the Christ arose
Triumphant over sin and death,
  A Victor over foes.

Angels of God announced, "Christ lives!
  The Lord of life is he";
They moved the stone that sealed the gave,
  And set death's prisoner free.

Because Christ lives we too shall live,
  His Word dispels our gloom;
He lights for us the shadowed vale,
  And lifts us from the tomb.

Hail then with joy this Easter morn,
  Rejoice; Rejoice and sing;
Around the world proclaim the news
  Of Christ, our Saviour King.

                  – Rev. Henry Felton Huse

"Thine Be The Dominion"

"We have no king but Caesar!"
  The jeering rabble cried.

Our king is Christ of Galilee
Whom then they crucified.
So many thrones have crumbled;
The Caesars turned to dust;
But he lives on forever,
The King in whom we trust.

The world is over-weary
Of wars that will not cease;
And now, as then, the Caesars
Have failed to bring us peace.

O Christ, our king eternal,
Come thou to rule and reign,
To end earth's desolation,
Here terrors, and her pain.

— Leach Gunn

No Other Way

My Master Knew no other way
To bind me to His heart,
Till He was bound one cruel day,
Upon a cross apart.
And I had known no other source
Of hearth for my sin-ridden soul,
Had He not risen one Easter Day
To enter in – make it whole.

— M.E. Hunter

Easter Petitions

May we present the Easter story,
O Lord, in such a way
That those we teach may see the glory
Of that first Easter Day.
So clearly may we bring the message,
Of hope and life and joy,
That we will give the day's true meaning
To every girl and boy.

And let us put in song such gladness,
    Such note of triumph bring, –
That all will catch the Easter Spirit,
    As allelujahs ring.

        – Agnes Volentine

Dawn

Near the Dawn Mary went,
    Grief-led, to serve the dead;
Though the miracle seemed spent,
    Ye stricken know why Mary went.
Through the dawn Simon came.
    For him, the mock of a distant cock
Coiled a new a lash of flame;
    Ye faithless know why Simon came.
Down the dawn angels sped,
    Radiant flight out-winging light.
"Christ lives," they sang. "He that was dead."
    Ye deathless know why angels sped.

        – Miriam LeFevre Crouse

The Easter Angel's Words

(Intermediate Recitation)

1. They came to the garden at sunrise,
    In sorrow of heart and fear,
    And with wonder they heard the angel
    Say, "He is no longer here.
    Come, see the place where they laid Him.
    It is now but an empty prison.
    Then, fear not, ye women who love Him,
    Lo, Jesus, your Lord, has risen."

2. "O why have ye come to seek Him,
    Here lying among the dead?
    He is living this Easter morning,
    He has risen, as He said.
    Go tell the glad Easter tidings,
    That Jesus has burst His prison.

Then, fear not, ye women who love Him.
Lo, Jesus your Lord has risen."

3. And still on this Easter morning,
    As oft in the days of yore,
    The wonderful words of the angel
    Are told for our ears once more;
    For Jesus today is living,
    For us He has rent death's prison.
    Then, fear not, but trust in His power.
    Lo, Jesus, your Lord, has risen."

Bible "Fear Nots"

(Junior Exercise)

1. God said to Paul when danger loomed,
    "Fear not, your life I'll save,
    With all your shipmates too"; and so Paul
    trusted and was brave.

2. When Abraham reached an unknown land,
    As God called him to do,
    God said, "Fear not"; and blessing came
    As Abraham trusted, too.

3. When Moses must lead Israel's host,
    God said, "Fear not," and lo,
    He trusted, and grew great and strong,
    The leader that we know.

4. When Joshua must strive and fight
    The Promised land to win,
    God said, "Fear not, I'll be your help"
    And Joshua entered in.

5. When Mary heard God's plan for her,
    Told by the angel guest,
    He said, "Fear not," and trusting,
    She was o'er all women blest.

6. When Bethlehem shepherds were afraid,
    "Fear not," God's angel said;
    And they, believing, found with joy
    Christ in His manger bed.

7. When we, too, face hard things, God says,
   "Fear not: I'll give you aid":
   And we, though trusting, can succeed
   And never be afraid.
8. "Be not afraid, . . .
   For the Lord thy God is with thee . . ."
   (Joshua 1:9)

Easter Offerings

Said Mother Nature, "Children dear,
Glad Easter day is drawing near.
Now what fair offerings will you bring
To greet the birthday of the spring?"

The blossoms answered: "We'll adorn
The brown earth for the Easter morn,
And breathe upon the fresh spring air,
Like incense, fragrance rich and rare."

The breezes said: "On soft wings fleet
We'll carry sounds and odors sweet,
And happy news with joy will bring,
For we're the messengers of spring."

The little birds sand loud: "And we
Her joyous orchestra will be,
Our clearest notes, in accents sweet,
Shall rise, spring's Easter day to greet."

And on the happy Easter day
Each one, in his own joyous way,
Blithe bird and breeze and blossom, told
The Easter story, sweet and old.

MISSIONARY MATERIAL

A Missionary Message

We send our love to every land;
True neighbors would we be;
And pray God's peace to reign in them,

Where'er their homeland be.
O God, to us may grace be given,
Who bear the dear Christ's name,
To live at peace with every man,
And thus our Christ acclaim.

– Ernest Bourner Allen, D.D.

What We Think

Recitation for Four Little Folks

1. I can't go across the sea,
    Because my mamma can't spare me;
    So I'll stay here and work and pray
    For little children far away.
2. I'll save all my nicest toys
    For little heathen girls and boys.
    Do children there know how to play?
    And do they "dress up" every day?
3. I wonder if there mammas love them;
    And do they have blue skies above them?
    And have they dolls and kittens, too?
    And have they flags red, white, and blue?
4. If they can't go to Sunday-school
    And learn about the Golden Rule,
    I don't see how they'll ever do
    What Jesus really wants them to!

Praying and Paying

Now isn't it funny! When people have money
    To spend on themselves every day,
    Why are they so sure to be too poor
    To do more for missions than pray?

It's only quite fair to back up one's prayer
    With money and service to;
    Prayers are all right; but a pocket book tight
    Won't help much to get them through.
And if there are any who can't give a penny

For the Gospel work in our land,
Then how can they go to the picture show?
I really don't quite understand;

If we'd pay as we pray, and work every day
To send the glad tidings around,
The world would be bright with Jesus'
own light,
And peace and good will could abound.

A Smile

– T.N. Tattersall

A smile played a great part in Livingstone's life. Though but a boy of 15, he had long cherished the dream of serving Christ as a missionary, and one November night went with his father to hear a deputation from the London Missionary Society in the Music Hall, Aberdeen. After the meeting he stood by the door, and when the deputation appeared he regarded them wistfully. The look on his face attracted the attention of Mr. Arthur, a Congregational minister, who turned to him with a smile and said:

"Well, my boy, would you like to be a missionary?"

"The smile," said his biographer, more than the words won him; he used afterwards to say that "it was that smile that made him a missionary."

– The Watchword

A Missionary Prayer for Brotherhood Transcending All Differences

Almighty Father, we who are members of different races and faiths, desire together to worship thy holy name in fellowship with each other. Thou art our Father, and we are thy children, show us that our hopes and fears and aspirations are one. Forgive, O God, the envy, suspicions and misunderstandings which have blinded our eyes and thrust us asunder. Purify our hearts and teach us to walk together in the laws of thy commandments and in the ways of human friendship.

– Joseph Fort Newton

Livingstone and The Children

(Missionary Playlet)

HERALD: Even after America was settled, and big towns were growing up, there were other countries where the children had never heard about Jesus. Especially in Africa men did not know about God. So David Livingstone went into the very heart of Africa and told the men and women and the children about Jesus. We want to show you in a little scene how David Livingstone loves the people of Africa and of how they came to love him.

(Chusa and his two little sisters enter)

CHUSA: I will talk to this white man and see if I may work for him. Maybe he will give us something to eat.

MWEMBA: But who will look after us while you are gone, Chusa? And where shall we stay?

CHUSA: (This is rather a blow to Chusa, but he is determined to find a way out.) I will take you along!

MWEMBA: I could go, maybe, but sister is too small.

CHEOLA: I am hungry, Chusa.

MWEMBA: (wistfully) We are always hungry, Chusa.

CHEOLA: When will mother come back, Mwemba?

CHUSA: (sadly) Never. The slave-raiders have taken her far away. (Consoling her) But I will look after you, Cheola.

MWEMBA: Maybe this white man will have a plan!

CHUSA: He is a great man. What will he care about three orphans?

MWEMBA: I shall ask him.

CHUSA (shaking his head) No! Then he might not give me service.

CHEOLA: (wailing) I am hungry!

CHUSA: Hush, little sister. There he comes. I will stop him and ask for a place in his service. Get back out of sight.

(Cheola and Mwemba sit down to one side, and Livingstone come in.)

CHUSA: (stopping him) Bwana –. (His courage fails)

LIVINGSTONE: (stopping and looking at him) What is it, lad?

CHUSA: I would work for food.

LIVINGSTONE: Where is your father? You are too little to work.

CHUSA: A year past the slave-raiders from the north took him and my mother also, I hid!

LIVINGSTONE: (sits down on a log and draws the boy to him; speaking very kindly) What can such a small boy do in my service?

CHUSA: I have done service as a broom.

LIVINGSTONE: (puzzled) As a broom?

CHUSA: Bwana, when the dew is very heavy on the long grass and the trail is wet, I will go before the caravan and shake the grass as I go. So will the dew fall and the caravan and the men remain dry.

LIVINGSTONE: And you?

CHUSA: (shivering a bit) It is cold – and wet. But presently the sun comes up and I am warmed and – and – it is better than an empty stomach.

LIVINGSTONE: Such a little lad!

CHEOLA: (wailing) I am hungry.

CHUSA: Bwana, they are my sisters.

LIVINGSTONE: And while thou art in my service, who cares for them?

CHUSA: Bwana, I do not know. (Troubled) Bwana, I do not wish them to die. What shall I do?

LIVINGSTONE: When did you eat?

CHUSA: A day and a night ago.

LIVINGSTONE: Go to my tent, son, and fetch food.

(Chusa goes. Livingstone calls the sisters. They come to him. Chusa returns with a broad smile and three bananas.)

LIVINGSTONE: Eat!

(Mwemba and Cheola star eating hungrily, but Chusa puts his aside.)

LIVINGSTONE: Why do you not eat, boy?

CHUSA: They will be hungry again soon. (Apologetically) Cheola is so little. I am not very hungry.

LIVINGSTONE: I take thee into my service, son, and the little sisters shall say with my people and be fed and clothed until thy return.

CHUSA: Bwana! But I cannot make enough to clothe and feed us all!

LIVINGSTONE: There is no need.

CHUSA: I will run in the wet grass all day long!

LIVINGSTONE: (smiling) In the early morning thou shalt lead the caravan. In the evenings thou shalt sit by the fire, and I will tell thee the stories of the Saviour who loves all little children, even such as thou and thy little sisters here.

CHUSA: (awestruck) You mean yourself, Bwana?

LIVINGSTONE: (smiling and shaking his head) No, lad, but stories of Jesus, who blessed the little children and taught us that God is our Father.

CHUSA: Bwana, do you know him?

LIVINGSTONE: I have known him for a long time, Chusa — and loved Him.

CHUSA: If he is like you, then I will love him, too.

LIVINGSTONE: Come, let us take the little sisters to the mission house and find a home and a mother for them.

CHUSA: (proudly) Come, little sisters, for behold, I am in the service of the Bwana, and he loves all little children! (They go out together.)

A Missionary Pledge of Brotherhood

God being my Father and all men being my brothers, I make this declaration:

1. I intend to do unto others, of whatever race or creed, as I would have them do unto me.

2. It is my purpose to respect the rights of human beings, and to judge each fellowman on his individual merits done.

3. I will oppose every organized effort to evoke fear or hatred of any religious or racial group.

Vitamins Most Vital

CHARACTERS: THE CHURCH – A man in somber attire, walking on crutches; DR. INTELLIGENCE – Middle aged or older man; VITAMINS – A, B, C, D, and E; SETTING: Doctor's Office.

THE CHURCH: What's wrong with me? What's wrong with me? I stay in my place and try to keep quiet. Am I getting too old for any good use? Or is there something amiss in my diet?

DR. INTELLIGENCE: Well, I just can't tell off-hand. You're a new patient, although I've treated many that had symptoms like you. I'll call in my assistants, then when you see what a good, healthy church needs, you can write your own prescription.

(Rings bell. Enter young woman in white gown, carrying Bible in one hand, and a large gold letter "A" in the other).

VITAMIN A: I am Vitamin A. I supply the vision of the church. Without me there is much stumbling in the darkness. I am the protective vitamin. If I am present, no degenerating disease is liable to gain foothold. With me there are not thin-skinned churches, for I give beauty to the soul, beauty which penetrates the surface and shines through the eyes. The church which takes me regularly lives a vigorous, normal life.

THE CHURCH: But where can I get you? Are you expensive?

VITAMIN A: Yes. You may have to make a few sacrifices at first in order to get me and keep me, but the greater the quantities in which you take me, the less I cost. I have another name. It is Worship. It must be quiet where I am, except when there are prayers, music and Scripture. I must be the supreme reason for church attendance. I should be taken home with every member and used daily, but so many people are careless and leave me lying in their pews till the next Sabbath. (Exit)

DOCTOR: (Rings Bell)

(Enter young girl or boy in a gray crepe paper hat, carrying a large red letter "B".)

VITAMIN B: I am Vitamin B. I aid in the church's digestion not only at church suppers, but when anything goes wrong – churches with my help can "take it." Though honestly, where I am, not many things seem to go wrong. I give the church room to breath. But the pep enters into its work. And the more you work, the more of me you need.

THE CHURCH: You sound good to me. Where can I get you?

VITAMIN B: A good way to order me is through your Young People's Society. My middle name is "Fun." Of course some adult should see that I'm not taken in too large a dose, but like Vitamin A, I'm needed all through the week by young and old alike, and the church should keep plenty of me in its supply cupboard. Some dealers will want to sell your young people "Thrills" in place of me, but tell them to insist on good healthy "Fun" and to accept no substitutes. (Exit)

DOCTOR: (Rings Bell)

(Enter young woman in choir robe, carrying the large purple letter "C.")

VITAMIN C: I am Vitamin C. I keep the church young. My presence insures a fine healthy, blood stream. Wounds heal more quickly and there are not fatal hemorrhages.

THE CHURCH: You sound necessary to my well-being. Are you hard to get?

VITAMIN C: No. In fact, most every church has some of me, but I have so many forms, you should be very careful in using me. In your worship, in your Sabbath School, in the nursery, in the Young People's Society, in pep and social meetings – I add much to all of these, if thought is given to my selection and if you have a capable person to administer me. You know me by the name of Music. (Exit)

DOCTOR: (Rings Bell)

(Enter young woman carrying the large purple letter "D".)

VITAMIN D: I am Vitamin D. Without me you have a weak-spined, knock-kneed, bow-legged church. In fact its whole structure will be deformed.

THE CHURCH: Certainly that should not be. How could we do without you?

VITAMIN D: Well, some churches try to, but without much success. You see I am the Spirit of Missions. I must first be taken directly into the heart, before I can be of much widespread good. Women have been the most faithful in using me, but the men need me every bit as much. If you can get the little children to accept me, and grow up with me, the future of your church is assured. Put a little of me into every Sabbath School lesson and have the minister at least flavor his sermon with me. (Exit)

DOCTOR: (Rings Bell)

(Enter young men in cap and gown, with diploma in hand and a large blue letter "E" in the other.)

VITAMIN E: I am Vitamin E. I make coordination in the church. If I am present, your church's muscles work as you want them to.

THE CHURCH: We certainly need you. Where can you be found?

VITAMIN E: I am Education or Instruction in Living. You get me mainly in your Church School, Summer Assemblies and Week Day Education groups. Trained consecrated teachers and leaders are the life stream in which I thrive. (Exit)

DR. INTELLIGENCE: And now, Patient Church, what do you say?

THE CHURCH: So many things are wrong with me

Who always should be in the right
But mine is not a hopeless case
For I begin to see the light.
With prayer and work must I be clothed,
With love my willing feet be shod –
That all I am or hope to be
Shall exist to the glory of God.

(CURTAIN)

MISSIONS
The Compelling Power of the Christian's Life

What is a Christian, anyhow? Isn't it about time someone was raising that question? This writer does not claim exceptional opportunities for observation and certainly not exceptional ability to interpret observations, but, for what it is worth, it is his deliberate judgment that Christ had less influence among his professed followers right now than in any period with which we are familiar. Without enumeration here, let the reader count the loyalties in the average Christian's life that take precedence over his loyalty to Christ. One may be able, for instance, to anticipate the position that a man will taken on a great public question by the party to which he belongs, the country club of which he is a member, the social set with which he runs, the bank with which he does business, or the gang with which he plays poker; but in too many cases it will not throw any light on the question to know what church he belongs to. In the third or fourth year of financial distress we are farther away from God than we were when the depression began. In fact, so far as our knowledge goes we have taken no steps as individuals or as a people to get right with God and thus to expect a return of his favor upon us. Sometimes we think our trouble lies in our neglect of our main business as Christians, and the corresponding depletion of our virility and resources. Missions, or witnessing for Christ to the ends of the earth, have always been the major task of Christians and the compelling power of their lives; to disregard this task is to invite the disasters that always follow in the train of powerless lives. We could call our people back to first things.

Missions? The Consuming Passion of the Heart of God

It is well enough to remember that man did not invent missions; missions were born of love – even the love of God himself. Glorious as is the record of the multitudes who have given their all in the service of missions, it is even more glorious that God conceived the idea and launched the plan. It was God that limited missions by the confines of His creation; He knows not the limits of territorial or racial boundaries, He includes the world in His love. How unbecoming it is for citizens of our country, the beneficiaries of foreign missions, to assume the attitude of favored people and to become indifferent to the spread of the gospel to which we owe our greatness. As the crowning evidence of the passion of the Father's heart, He gave expression to it in the gift of His Son to be the Saviour of the world. Jesus is at once the price of man's redemption and the measure of God's love.

Missions: The Guiding Principle in the Motive of Jesus

We are not left in doubt as to the motive of Jesus in coming to earth. "My meat is to do the will of him that sent me." "I lay down my life for the sheep." "For the Son of man came to seek and to save that which was lost." Such sayings could be multiplied many times – all of them revealing that missions were the guiding principle in the purpose of Jesus.

Furthermore, His living service on earth confirms the same fact. Follow Him throughout His compassion, go out to all needy and sinful ones – the leper by the roadside, the paralytic by the pool, the woman in the public place; everywhere the redemptive mission of Jesus was in evidence. Of course, His matchless sacrifice crowned His motive. His humiliation, His shame, His death – all leave no doubt at all as to the guiding principle of the Master.

It is enough to be like God and Jesus.

Missions: The Public Confirmation of Christian Profession

The supporter of missions demonstrates to the world that there is reality in his profession. Because he was once lost in sin, he would bring a message of hope to all sinners; because he has found salvation by the grace of Christ, he would gladly undertake to witness for him the world round by personal testimony and by the use of his means. There may be non-missionary Christians; there are no anti-missionary Christians. Thousands of Christians are non-missionary because they are uninformed or unenlisted, but no Christian can oppose missions. Justice to our brethren demands frankness here. The world looks for the practical expression of open profession; Christ depends upon faithful witnessing.

Missions: The Rational Condition To Christian Praying

Prayer becomes real when one is clearly in the will of Christ carrying out his commission; one cannot claim the promises of Christ unless he is walking in the will of Christ. The selfish can't pray; the socially arbitrary or exclusive can't pray; only the surrendered, devoted servant can walk in the will of God, which is praying. Only those who go and do in obedience to the command of the Lord can rest in the security of "Lo, I am with you always." Praying and going are hand in hand. William Carey was right when he said, "Missions make prayer rational."

We Are All Brothers

The One bethought Him to make man
Of many-colored dust,
And mixed the holy spirit in
In portions right and just;
Each had a part of mind and heart.
From One Himself in trust.

Thus came the brown and yellow men
And black and white and red,
So different in their outer look
Alike in heart and head;
The self-same earth before their birth,
The self-same dust when dead.

— A poem by Confucius

Acrostic Reading

For the acrostic reading select four little girls for "H-O-M-E," three smaller ones for "A-N-D," seven boys for "F-O-R-E-I-G-N," and eight of the larger girls for "M-I-S-S-I-O-N-S," giving to each a verse or text beginning with the letter assigned.

Black letters on stiff white cardboard should be used, suspended by a ribbon around the neck, the wearer coming upon the platform when it is time for his letter. The one having H recites first, followed by the one having O, etc., until the world H-O-M-E is spelled from right to left facing the audience. Next, the three smaller girls recite their texts in the same manner, spelling the word A-N-D, standing a few feet farther forward, as per diagram. Then the boys, one at a time, with verse and letter, until the word F-O-R-E-I-G-N is spelled. The larger girls have larger letters for M-I-S-S-I-O-N-S, and stand on a higher platform unless they are much taller than those spelling the other words.

All should remain on the platform throughout the singing of "The Gospel Banner" and "The Morning Light is Breaking." A large banner, with the inscription, "The World for Christ," would be appropriate as a background. The following diagram may be useful:

A-N-D
M-I-S-S-I-O-N-S
(Front of Platform)

Four Girls

H ome is the dearest spot on earth, wherever it
may be;

O urs is the greatest home of all – this land so
bright and free.

M any people, scattered wide, need tidings, Lord,
of Thee;

E ach one is dear to Thy great heart, wherever
He may be.

Three Girls

A nd they shall be mine, saith the Lord of hosts,
in that day when I make up my jewels.

N o good thing will He withhold from them that
walk uprightly.

D o unto others as ye would that others should
do unto you.

Seven Boys

F rom far across the sea there comes a cry for
life and light;

O n many shores, in many lands, their brightest
day is night.

R eveal to us who have Thy light what we must
do, O Lord;

E ach one may help with willing heart, by prayer
or smile or word.

I n Thy dear name we ask, O Lord, what Thou
wouldst have us do;

G ive each the mind to work for Thee; our
courage oft renew.

N ew light for lands in darkness veiled we ask to
send afar;

Till every land shall worship Thee, and follow Bethlehem's star.

– Carrie B. Adams

Eight Girls

M y praise shall be of Thee in the great
congregation. All the ends of the world shall
remember and turn unto the Lord; and all
the kindred of the nations shall worship
before Thee.

I am come a light into the world, that whosoever
believeth on me should not abide in
darkness.

S how me Thy ways, O Lord; teach me Thy
paths. Lead me in Thy truth and teach me.

S ay unto them that are of a fearful heart, Be
strong; fear not. Behold your God will come
with a recompense. He will come and save
you.

I n this was manifested the love of God, because
that God sent His only begotten Son into the
world, that we might live through Him.

O how great is Thy goodness, which Thou hast
laid up for them that fear Thee.

N ot unto us, O Lord, not unto us, but unto Thy
name give glory, for Thy mercy, and for Thy
truth's sake.

S o teach us to number our days, that we may
apply our hearts unto wisdom.

Missionary Reading

How beautiful upon the mountains are the feet of him that
bringeth good tidings; that publish peace; that bringeth
good tidings of good; that publisheth salvation; that said
unto Zion Thy God reigneth.

For ye shall go out with joy, and be led forth with peace; the
mountains and the hills shall break forth before you into

singing, and all the trees of the fields shall clap their hands.

Then shall the eyes of the blind be opened, and the ears of the deaf unstopped.

And the ransomed of the Lord shall return, and come with singing unto Zion; and everlasting joy shall be upon their heads; and they shall obtain gladness and joy, and sorrow and sighing shall flee away.

A Smile

– T.N. Tattersall

A smile played a great part in Livingstone's life. Though but a boy of 15, he had long cherished the dream of serving Christ as a missionary, and one November night he went with his father to hear a deputation from the London Missionary Society in the Music Hall, Aberdeen. After meeting he stood by the door, and when the deputation appeared he regarded them wistfully. The look on his face attracted the attention of Mr. Arthur, a Congregational minister, who turned to him with a smile and said:

"Well, my boy, would you like to be a missionary?"

"The smile," said the biographer, more than the words won him; he used afterwards to say that is was that smile that made him a missionary." – The Watchword.

> We send our love to every land;
> True neighbors would we be;
> And pray God's peace to reign in them,
> Where'er their homeland be.
> O God, to us may grace be given,
> Who bear the dear Christ's name,
> To live at peace with every man,
> And thus our Christ acclaim.

– Ernest Bourner Allen, D.D.

Africa's Cry

"At last my hard-earned check has come,
    And I am off to town,
To buy the book I've waited for,
    The blouse I saw marked down;
Or else, perhaps, a pair of gloves –
    I think I need them more;
So, dallying with my petty wants,
    I reached the tempting store.
As I waited for the clerk,
    Browsing on magazines,
My eye was fixed by starving eyes;
    Down fell the veil that screens
Our sight from vision.
    There I saw Upon far Africa's beach
A starving mother with her flock
    Gazing beyond her reach
For food that did not come;
    No sail uploomed on the drear sea.
"In God's name, do not let them die!"
    I heard her call to me.
Oh, no, I do not want the book;
    My eyes are blind with tears;
And still, among the silken stuffs,
    That cry assails my ears;
And waxen arms stretch trembling
    Wherever I would buy.
My check – in God's name save one child,
    And soothe one bitter cry."

The Least of These

A child is crying beyond our door
    In the cold and wind and the wild downpour,
How can we sit at east within?
    A child is calling beyond our gate,

Starving and stark and desolate,
    How can we bid the feast begin?
How may we sit content and warm
    When a child is lost in the night and storm?
The night of famine, the storm of war,
    How may we break our bread in ease,
Hearing the voice of the least of these?
    A child is crying beyond our door.

MOTHER'S DAY MATERIAL

Welcome

(A recitation by a small boy or girl)

Of all the lovely holidays
That gladden all the year
Mother's Day is at the top –
And we're so glad you're here!

The Origin of Mother's Day

Many years ago the English set aside a day for honoring their mothers. It was observed on Mid-Lent Sunday and was known as Mothering Sunday. Everyone was expected to attend his mother church – the church in which he had been baptized and raised – and to visit his parents, taking a gift. The traditional gift of the day was a simnel cake, baked of the best wheat flour obtainable.

Only in comparatively recent times, however, has a special day for mothers been observed in the United States.

Although there are conflicting claims, Miss Anna Jarvis, of Philadelphia, Pennsylvania, is generally given credit for the establishment of Mother's Day as we know it.

In 1907, Miss Jarvis was asked to arrange a memorial service for her mother who had, prior to her death, been an active member and a moving spirit in her church. As Miss Jarvis made plans for the service, she realized more and more the growing lack of tenderness and consideration for their mothers on the part of grown-up children, especially those who were living away from home. So in that service Miss Jarvis made a plea that some Sunday in each year be set aside as a memorial to mothers. Acting upon her suggestion, the city of Philadelphia designated May 10, 1908, as Mother's Day.

In 1912, the states of Washington and Oklahoma observed Mother's Day on May 12 by proclamations of the governors. The following year, both houses of the United States Congress passed resolutions recommending the observance of the day. On May 8, 1914, Congress passed a bill authorizing the President to set aside by proclamation a day to be known as Mother's Day. The next day, President Wilson designated the second Sunday in May to be observed.

Special services are held in all churches and flags are displayed on every government building on Mother's Day, the day set aside to honor "the best mother in all the world – your own."

– Harry A. Tritt

Helpful Thoughts

If I obey in little things,
And do them with a smile –
I'll find it isn't hard to do
The big things after while.

– Mary Agnes Colville

To Mother Dear

To you, Mother dear, on Mother's Day
I give a loving heart,
I give you happiness as well,
In which I have a part.

All year I've done my very best
In school, at home, and play,
Because to make you happy, dear,
I know that is the way.

I've earned good marks, I've helped you too,
No quarrels marred my play,
And so, with love, I give to you,
A happy Mother's day!

Mother

My mother does the nicest things
For me every day;
She always makes me want to sing,
As I work and play.

–Maxie Lee Broadwell

Prayer for Mother's Day

O God, we thank Thee for the gifts
That come from Thee alone,
And chiefly for the mother love
Which is so like Thine own.
The love that shields our infancy,
The love that guides our youth;
That shows the wonders of Thy law,
The glories of Thy truth.
We pray that Thou wilt greatly bless
Our mothers in this day
With treasures from Thy heavenly store
That cannot pass away.
We pray that sons and daughters
May ever loyal be,
And may our mothers' prayers fulfill
By truly serving Thee.

Helping Mother

Your hands may be small, but every day
They can do something that's good as play;
They can help mother, and she'll be glad
For all that's done by her lass or lad.

If all the children would think today
Of helping mother, as all of them may,

They'd bring in water and wood, and do
A dozen things she would like them to.

For, though hands are small and years are few,
There's always something that they can do
To help the mothers and make them glad;
Remember that, little lass and lad.

So help your mothers about their work;
Don't wait for asking – don't try to shirk.
Do just the best that you can, and she
Will say, "What a help are my dears to me!"

Christian Mother

There glows an ageless beauty in her face,
A gentleness in all her wondrous ways
With quite strength she daily finds her place.
And serves without a thought of praise.

She has a poise that only those can know
Whose hearts have suffered long, have bled;
And yet with quiet courage bravely go
To share the tears other in sorrow shed.

It matters not how dark the night; how long;
What storms of anguish come, or tempests roll,
Safe from them all will ever be the song
Of faith that burns within her noble soul.

– Selected

The Light On My Mother's Face

Oh, many years have passed away
Since Mother's voice was stilled,
And yet, I seem to hear her pray
Her voice my soul has filled.
Each morn behind that fast closed door
Her pleading voice I'd hear
In joy, and oft in anguish sore,
She'd speak to some One near,
Her little room was filled with praise,

She softly spoke his name.
And Oh, the light upon her face
When from that room she came.
That light, that smile, they faded not
But lasted all day through
And made our home a sunlit spot
Where heavenly flowers grew.

Oh, times may change, and days may go,
And knowledge grow apace,
But never, never shall I know
A more illumined face
Than that my precious mother wore
Out from the sacred hour
When she in joy and anguish sore
Called on her Friend of power.
O God, I thank Thee for her life
And sacred memory.
As she, may I, in joy and strife
For e'er abide in Thee.
God, Thou hast drawn me all my days
From tender years till now,
Because the light on mother's face
Revealed Thy wondrous power.

– Esther Anderson Steen

The Little Mother

Now, Dolly, dear, I'm going away,
And want you to be good all day.
Don't lose your shoes nor soil your dress,
Not get your hair all in a mess.
But lie quite still, and up I'll come,
To kiss you soon as I come home.
I'd take you, dear, but then you know,
It's wax Sabrina's turn to go
She sick, I'm 'fraid. Her eyes don't work;
They open worse, the more I jerk;

She used to be so straight and stout,
But now her sawdust's running out.
Her kid is out of order, dear.
My papa says she's out of gear.
That's dreadful, isn't it? But then
The air may make her well again
So, Dolly, won't you stay alone,
And be real good while I am gone?
Goodbye, my precious! Yes, I'll come
And kiss you soon as I get home.

–Frank Leslie's Boys and Girls' Weekly

Remembering Mother

The garden smiles on Mother's Day,
With roses all abloom;
I always pick a big bouquet
To put in mother's room.

And as I pass the easy chair
Where mother used to sit,
And as I pass the easy chair
When ev'ning lamps were lit.

I take her Bible in my hand
From its accustomed shelf;
And sitting down in mother's chair
I read a page myself.

I think of all that mother was,
And wanted me to be;
How kind she was to ev'ry one,
How much she did for me!

No better way I know, than this,
For keeping Mother's Day;
And so I sit and read the Book
That guided mother's way.

– Margery Isabel

A Prayer for A Mother

Lord, I thank you for my Mother,
For her loving tender care;
And I ask that you be with her,
Help her all her burdens bear.

Guide her steps where're she wanders,
In the home so dear to me;
May she feel you ever near her;
May she always trust in Thee.

I thank the Lord, that she hast taught me,
Of the Christ so kind and true
Of His blood He shed on Calvary,
And His Resurrection, too.

May I not forget to thank her,
For her prayers that do ascend;
May her prayers receive an answer,
This I pray for her – Amen.

– Ellen B. Price

The Tie of Love

One day, one of the gigantic eagles of Scotland carried away a sleeping infant. The whole village pursued it, but the eagle soon perched itself upon a lofty crag and every one despaired of the child's life.

A sailor tried to climb the ascent, but he was obliged to give up the attempt. A robust Highlander, accustomed to hill climbing, tried but was forced to return. At last a poor peasant woman came forward and putting her feet on one shelf of the rock, then a second, then a third, she rose to the very top of the cliff. While the hearts of those below were trembling, she came down step by step, until amid the shouts of the villagers, she stood at the bottom of the rock with the child on her bosom.

Why did that woman succeed when the strong sailor and the practiced Highlander failed? Why? Because between her and the babe there was a tie; that woman was the mother of the babe. Let there be that tie of love of Christ and to souls in your heart, and greater wonders will be accomplished.

– King's Business

Mother's Day

I. A Mother's Care: Exodus 2:3, 4; 2 Timothy 3:15

Both Moses and Timothy had godly mothers who tenderly cared for them. When Moses was born, his life was in danger, and he was hidden three months, during which time he was under his mother's loving care. When she could no longer hide him she placed him in an ark and laid it in the flags by the river's brink.

By faith, she committed him into God's care, and in a wonderful way He met her faith, and permitted her to care for her child again. Her tender care left a lasting impression for good upon her boy. In after years he was wonderfully used of God in caring for His chosen people.

Timothy's mother was very faithful in training her boy in the way of the Lord. When but a child, she taught him in the holy scriptures; 2 Timothy 3:15. Early in life he accepted Christ as his Saviour, and became a preacher of the gospel. If there were more faithful mothers, like Eunice, there would be more Bible knowledge, conversions, and ministers of the gospel. Children will never forget the Bible stories that were told them, in their youth by their mothers, and as a result, many have in after years been led to Christ. How many parents fail to take time to read and explain the Word of God to their children; no wonder that they neglect their soul's salvation and disrespect the Word of God.

II. A Mother's Prayers: Mark 7:26; Matthew 15:25

The Syrophenician woman had a great burden on her heart. Her daughter was vexed with a devil and she came to Jesus for help. She received no encouragement at first; the disciples wanted Jesus to send her away, but she paid no attention to this, but pleaded all the more. She was willing to take the place of a dog, just so she could get a few crumbs from Jesus' table. Her prayers were answered, and her daughter was delivered. Thank God for mothers who know how to pray through, and will not take "no" for an answer. There are many mothers whose names have never been published but they have been a mighty power for good in this sinful world, because they have lived lives of prayer. Some have never traveled much, but they have gone around the world thousands of times, in their prayers. Some have never preached the Word in public, but they have sent out a host of preachers through prayer. Some are invalids – shut ins, but through their intercessions, heaven's blessing is falling upon the dry ground.

Many years ago there was a mother in Somerville, New Jersey, whose son, a young man, had begun to lead a dissolute life. One evening she begged him not to spend that evening away from her, but he declared that he would. He said; "Mother, I'm not going to be tied to your apron string; I am going to go." The mother replied, "Please try and remember every moment tonight that, until you come back, I'm going to be on my knees asking God to save you." The son, with a rude gesture and muttered oath, rushed from her presence and spent the night in a shameful carousal. It was four o'clock in the morning when he got home. As he got to the house he saw a light shining through the shutters. Turning the blinds down and looking in, he saw his mother on her knees, and heard her pray, "God save my wandering boy." Going to his room he threw himself on his bed, but he could not sleep. After awhile he arose, then he knelt down, and it seemed to him as though Christ's power proceeded from the room where his wrestling mother was pleading with God, and it led him to cry out, "God be merciful to me a sinner." And that very morning he was saved.

III. A Mother's Love: Isaiah 49:15; John 19:25

D.L. Moody says, "The strongest human love that we know of is a mother's love. Many things will separate a man from his wife. A father may turn his back on his child; brothers and sisters may become inveterate enemies; husbands may desert their wives; wives their husbands. But a mother's love endures through all. In good repute, in bad repute, in the face of the world's condemnation, a mother loves on, and hopes that her child may turn from his evil ways and repent. She remembers the infant smiles, the merry laugh of the childhood, the promise of youth; and she can never be brought to think him unworthy. Death cannot quench a mother's love; it is stronger than death. You have seen a mother watching over her sick child. How willingly she would take the disease into her own body if she could thus relieve the child! Week after week she will keep watch; she will let no one else take care of that sick child. A friend of mine, some time ago, was visiting in a beautiful home where he met a number of friends. After they had all gone away, having left something behind, the went back to get it. There he found the lady of the house, a wealthy lady, sitting behind a poor fellow who looked like a tramp. He was her own son. Like the prodigal he had wandered far away; yet the mother said, "This is my boy; I love him still."

1. Tell something about the mother of Moses.
2. Tell something about Timothy's early training.
3. What lessons can we learn from the Syrophenician Woman?
4. Relate the answer of some mother's prayer.
5. Give some incidents of a mother's love.

Mother's Day

Who?

Who can tell us 'bout the flowers?
And the weeks and days and hours?

How the giant oak tree grows?
Mother – she knows.

Who will teach us how to pray,
At the close of each glad day,
When star-lighted heaven glows?
Mother – she knows.

Who loves us the very best,
Who goes with us to our rest,
And a good night kiss bestows?
Mother – she knows.

On Mother's Day

Gentle hands that never weary toiling in love's vineyard sweet,

Eyes that seem forever cheery when your eyes they chance to meet.

Tender, patient, brave, devoted, that is always mother's way,

Could her worth in gold be quoted as you think of her today?

There shall never be another quite so tender, quite so kind,

As the patient little mother, nowhere on this earth you'll find

Her affections duplicated none so proud if you are fine.

Could her worth be overstated? Not by any words of mine.

Death stood near the hour she bore us, agony was hers to know,

Yet she bravely faced it for us, smiling in her time of woe;

Down the years how oft we've tried her, often selfish, heedless, blind.

Yet with love alone to guide her, she was never once unkind.

Vain are all our tributes to her if in words alone they dwell.

We must live the praises due her; there's no other way to tell

Gentle Mother that we love her, would you say, as you recall

All the patient service of her, you've been worthy of them all?

Mother Dear

God sent the birds and sunshine
    To gladden all the world;
He sent the foliage and flowers
    In radiance unfurled;
He sent the June, the stars, the moon,
    The pearly dewdrops sweet
And then He sent you, Mother Dear
    To make it all complete.

His Mother's Faith

They said he would never amount to much,
    But his mother said he would;
That he never could set the river on fire,
    But his mother vowed he could.
They said of beauty he had not a trace,
    But his mother thought he had;
When they spoke of future Presidents
    She lovingly look at her lad.
But it happened as months and years went by
    This lad who was awkward and dull and shy,
Who never could set the river on fire,
    Attained the goal of his heart's desire,
And he gave glad thanks, while his eyes were
    dim,
Because of his mother's faith in him.

A Mother's Prayer

To teach my boy to live
That every deed shall be a breath of prayer
To teach him how the God who gives him life
Must honored be in loving ministry;
To teach him that true deed and noble strife
Will stand him eye to eye with any man –
This is my task, – and this true motherhood.

                     – M.E. Hunter

Careers

I've heard mother sigh: "Oh dear and Oh dear,
I do envy women who have a career!
A mother is only a seamstress, a nurse,
A custodian of a measly budget and purse;
A laundress and cook, a dietitian,
In an emergency, sometimes a physician,
A supervisor of play, a leader of youth,
An expert in styles, dispenser of truth,
A diplomat, teacher, companion and friend,
Counselor, critic – there is never an end,
To all a good and wise mother must be,
Nor to the scope of her ministry;
She's an arbitrator of strife and of peace,
By day and by night her tasks never cease . . . .
Other women, less favored, may have a career
In which they excel, but isn't it clear
By your own admission, when all's said and
    done,
That motherhood's every profession in one?

Helping Mother

(A Recitation for a very little girl)
I like to help my mother
    Set the table every day
And when the meal is over,
    I help put things away.
I always wipe the knives and forks,
    And lay them very straight,
And put a spoon most carefully
    By every person's plate.
My mother often says that I'm
    The best help ever was,
She smiles at me and praises me,
    And I am glad she does.

My Mother's Bible

(A Junior or Intermediate child holds his mother's Bible or a well-worn Bible in his hand as he recites.)

Mother's Bible, precious volume,
　　Doubly dear it seems to me
God has given it to His children:
　　It is Mother's gift to me.
"Holy Bible!" How I love it!
　　Mother loved it long ago
And she taught me in her closet
　　How to love this Bible too.
Mother's Bible, Holy Bible,
　　'Twas her guide from day to day;
Here she found a cheering cordial
　　When her loved ones passed away.
'Twas her comfort when in trouble,
　　'Twas her joy when sorrows came;
Mother loved this precious Bible
　　More than worldly worth and fame.
Mother's Bible, blessed Bible.
　　All its promises are true:
Mother saw them fully tested
　　Ere she bid this world adieu.
In the swelling of the river,
　　They sustained her even there;
"Christ is with me," mother whispered,
　　"Soon I shall His glory share."
Holy Bible, precious Bible,
　　Blessed book so dear to me;
Here I read sweet words of cheering,
　　From my mother's legacy.
Mothers, teach your little children,
　　While their tender hearts are pure;
Teach them now to love the Bible –
　　They will bless you evermore.

Making Mother Glad

God help each one of us to see
Just what our mothers need,
For is we know then we can make
Them very glad indeed.
Make each of us a ray of light,
A sunbeam on their way.
Help us to make the days all bright,
And each a Mother's day!

Loving Hands and Heart

Are you a willing helper
And always glad to do
The errands that your mother
Will sometimes ask of you?
And are you always willing
To leave your play a while
To do something for mother
And do it with a smile?
To be a willing helper
And each day do your part
You must be always ready
With loving hands and heart.

NEW YEAR'S DAY

A Resolution For The New Year

I'll say the loyal helpful thing that makes
life sweet and fair –
I'll pay the gratitude I owe for human love
and care.
Perhaps I've been at fault sometimes –
I'll ask to be forgiven
And make this little world of mine seem like a
bit of heaven.

Dialogue: The Old Year and The New

(For two children: One dressed as an old man with a scythe over his shoulder and one very small youngster with badge across his chest reaching under the arm and up over the other shoulder bearing the date of the New Year.)

Old Year says:

    Little New Year, you are fearfully small
    To carry this burden alone!
    Just how will you know just how you should go?
    There's so much to you should be shown.
    Your little soft feet will bruise on life's street,
    Your shoulders great burdens must bear,
    I fear that your heart will bleed and will smart
    At sorrow and pain you must share!

New Year says:

    Blessed Old Year, you are fearfully old,
    And truly, I'm glad you can go!
    For why should you bear earth's woe and its care
    When I am right here and I know
    There's joy and there's bliss I somehow can't miss,
    There's love, and small children at play,
    There are brides, there are grooms and silver boat moons
    And sunset at end of the day.

There Is No Path Ahead

    There is no path ahead this New Year's Day,
    No feet have trod this strange uncharted land
    That lies before my eyes . . . God, lead the way,
    God, take hold of my hand.
    I dare not go alone, the hills are steep,
    The distances are great, the valleys wide,
    I cannot travel them unless you keep
    Me close, Lord, by your side.

    There is no broken trail ahead today,
    No feet have gone the way that I must go.

Be my companion and my guide, I pray,
For with you, Lord, I know.

The hills will level as I come to them,
The valleys will be cool and sweet with dew,
And down the tangled ways each briar-hung stem
Will part to let me through.

Looking Ahead

The nice part of the New Year is the fact that it gives us a reason to look ahead. And looking ahead is, in more ways than one, a very satisfying pastime.

Too many of us have a bad habit of looking backwards to the hopes and the dreams that never came true. We worry about the parties to which we weren't invited, the examinations that we didn't pass, the club honors that fell to the lot of somebody else, and the wrong words that we have used at the wrong time, and of the right words that we have failed to use at the right time, of those things that we have done, and those other things that we have left undone!

Some of us look back to past happiness and past success. We look back to joyous days that have been filled with fun and laughter, days of summer picnics and winter skating parties, days when we were with friend and enjoyed ourselves. But no looking back, even to the happiest sort of an occasion, is as pleasant as looking forward to the things that may happen.

We can look ahead to ambitious things. To successes in school and to success of a more social nature. We can look ahead to the day next June when we will have passed all the tests and will face a long vacation. We can look ahead to the concert that will be held next week. We can look ahead to the class party, and we can hope to be the most popular girl there.

We can look ahead, also, to selfish things, but it doesn't help character building in the slightest. The selfish things to which we can look ahead are the pleasures that we don't wish to share. But in the final analysis, is an unshared pleasure really a pleasure? We can look ahead to clothes that are prettier than those worn by other girls. We can look ahead to marks so high that they will embarrass the less brilliant members of our class. We can look ahead to extravagant, expensive forms of entertainment that we do not deserve and cannot afford. But I'm sure that none of the girls who read this article will look forward in such a fashion!

I think rather that the girls who read this article will look ahead unselfishly. They will want nice clothes, but not clothes that will put to shame those worn by their associates. They will look ahead to good marks, but not for the sake of showing off. They will look ahead to popularity, but a popularity that is gracious and tolerant and that remembers what it feels like to be unpopular.

The girl who looks ahead unselfishly will plan to help her mother during the days and weeks and months that lie in the future. She will do her share of the housework and will uncomplainingly do more than her share. If her father is harassed by business cares and financial worries, she will not demand impossible things, for she will know that it is unkind and unfair for her to do so. After she had finished her homework she will help her small brother with his arithmetic, and she will not laugh at him because he is unable to solve the problem for himself. Last, but not least, she will realize that some day she herself will have a family and for that reason she'll try to do her part in making the family life run smoothly.

Of course, we can look beyond next year to a whole chain of years. We can look forward to happiness that is mature, and to pleasures that are based on sacrifice. We can look forward to a life of giving, and to the realization that giving is much more blessed than receiving. We can look forward to a life of service; service to others and service to the Most High.

When the new year arrives, and we're making our resolutions, we must make them wisely and honestly. We must pledge ourselves to look ahead in the bright way and the right way. We must not look ahead as if we were looking into a mirror, for a mirror only throws back our own reflection. We must look ahead in another fashion. We must imagine ourselves standing on a mountaintop gazing beyond fields, woods and valleys to a horizon line that has no end.

Looking ahead and dreaming must never be confused. For dreaming is playing with the filmy stuff of the imagination, and looking ahead is building with a sturdy stuff that, if handled correctly, can form a foundation for your whole life.

The nicest part of New Year's is the fact that it gives us a real reason to do this building!

Look ahead to gladness,
Making all things bright;
Look ahead to star-shine
Silvering the night;
Look ahead to beauty,
Look ahead to cheer,
Look ahead to happiness,
Through all the coming year!
Look ahead to sharing,
Look ahead to mirth;
Look ahead to helping
The sad ones of this earth.
Look ahead to friendship
And to family ties,
Look ahead to happiness,
The sort that never dies!

My Resolutions For This Year

1. As a Christian, I resolve to make this year a year of fruitful service to my Lord and Master. He shall find me faithful in whatever task I undertake.

2. I resolve to attend all the services of my church, unless providentially hindered: The preaching service, the teaching service, the training services and the prayer service.

3. Realizing my strength comes from the Lord, I resolve to set aside a definite period each day for Bible study, prayer and meditation on Holy things.

4. It shall be my purpose to better equip myself for my tasks, regardless of how small or large they may be. (If you have not place of service, your pastor, Training Union Director or Sunday School Superintendent will be happy to make a place for you.)

5. Definite reading and study shall have a place in my daily program.

6. From month to month I will plan my work because I know worthwhile things do not "just happen."

7. My few talents and many material blessings from God will be at His disposal. I will be a good steward.

"I Can Do All These Things Through Jesus Christ
Which Strengthenth Me" – Philippians 4:13.

"To leave the old with a burst of song,
To recall the right and forgive the wrong,
To forget the thing that binds you fast
To the vain regrets of the years far past;
To have the strength to let go your hold
Of the not worthwhile, of the days grown old,
To dare go forth with a purpose true,
To the unknown task of the year that's new;
To help your brother along the road
To do his work and lift his load;
To add your gift to the world's good cheer,
Is to have and to give a Happy New Year."

Road Map For A Year

Oh, who will make the road map for
The year that is so young?
A map to show where 'round the curve
Lace valentines are strung,
And where the Easter choruses
Are waiting to be sung,

85

And where upon the hill of spring
Bright Maypole ribbons fly
Just this side of the flowers of June
And flags that mark July,
And where the school bells sway anew
Against September's sky.
The map must point out Halloween's
Black-draped and clanging gates.
And mark a short cut leading through
Township Thanksgiving plates,
Past lighted Christmas trees, to where
Another New Year waits.

Recipe For A Happy New Year

Take twelve fine, full grown months, see that these are thoroughly free from all old memories of bitterness, rancor, hate, and jealousy; cleanse them completely from every clinging spite; pick off all specks of pettiness and littleness; in short; see that these months are free from all the past – have them as fresh and clean as when they first came from the storehouse of time.

Cut these months into 30 or 31 equal parts. This batch will keep for just a year. Do not attempt to make up the whole batch at one time (so many persons spoil the entire lot this way), but prepare one day at a time, as follows:

Into each day put 12 parts of faith, 11 of patience, 10 of courage, 9 of work (some people omit this ingredient and so spoil the flavor of the rest), eight of hope, seven of fidelity, six of liberality, five of kindness, four of rest (leaving this out is like leaving the oil out of the salad – don't do it), three of prayer, two of meditation, and one well-selected resolution. If you have no conscientious scruples, put in about a teaspoonful of good spirits, a dash of fun, a pinch of folly, a sprinkling of play, and a heaping cupful of good humor.

Pour into the whole love (and plenty of it) and mix with vim. Cook thoroughly in fervent heat; garnish with a few smiles and a sprig of joy; then serve with quietness, unselfishness, and cheerfulness, and a Happy New Year is a certainty.

The New Year

I am the New Year, and I come to you pure
  and unstained,
Fresh from the hand of God . . . .
I give you, free and unstinted, twelve glorious
  months,
Of soothing rain and sunshine golden;
The days for work and play, the nights for
  peaceful slumber
All that I ask – that you keep the faith
  unbroken!

Another Year

Another year is but another call from God
To do some deed undone and duty we forgot
To see and love with kindlier eyes and
  warmer heart,
Until, acquainted more with Him and keener
  eyed
To sense the need of man, we serve
With larger sacrifice and readier hand our
  kind.

A Wish For The New Year

May the New Year take naught away
You'd wish to have and hold;
But add some good gifts of its own
Before the year is old.

New Year Quips

I wish you a Happy New Year,
  I pray its course may bring

A calm contentment to your heart –
Life's richest offering.

"De man dat succeeds," said Uncle Eben, "is de man dat has de grit to get up every mornin' an' put ditto marks under his New Year resolutions."

The year begins. Let us begin with high resolution: then let us take all its hindrances, its disappointments, its narrow and commonplace conditions, and meet them as the Master did in Nazareth, with patience, with obedience, putting ourselves in cheerful subjection, serving our apprenticeship. Who knows what opportunity may come to us this year? Let us live in a great spirit, then we shall be ready for a great occasion.

– George Hodges

Goodbye, kind year; we walk no more together
But here in quiet happiness we part,
And from thy wreath of faded fern and heather
I take some sprays and wear them on my heart.
– Sarah Doudney

Blessed is this year in its coming and going, most
beautiful, because it is the year of our Lord.
– Lucy Larcom

O year that is coming, bring with you
Some virtue of which I have need;
More patience to bear,
And more kindness to share,
And more love that is true love indeed.
– Laura Armitage

New Year's Day

When New Year's time comes around we can't help feeling a certain thrill. It is a thrill that is different from any other holiday thrill. It isn't like the excitement that is a part of birthdays, or the expectancy that belongs to Christmas, when we expect to receive something. It isn't like

Thanksgiving when we know prayer and feasting and the sensation of gratitude. It isn't even like the thrill that marks Halloween, a time of unadulterated fun.

New Year's Day gives us a thrill because it is an open door to the new year. We tell ourselves – and rightly – that anything can happen in the new year. We may go anywhere, or do anything, or meet anybody. It's adventurous – is New Year's Day – with the finest sort of adventure. It's breathlessly lovely, too, because it gives us a chance to express ourselves in the matter of resolutions and pledges.

I have known people who celebrated each New Year's Day by writing long lists of resolutions on long sheets of white paper. Some of these resolutions they have kept during the year, and some they early set aside. I've known other people who have written only one or two resolutions in the secret places of their hearts, but these few resolutions they have scrupulously kept. I think the heart resolutions – which are made to be kept – are the best ones. And most of these best ones, in one way or another, are inspired by the Golden Rule.

At The Gate

The gate is ajar into New Year Land,
Open to us by an unseen hand,
The hand of the Father, who led us here,
Into the realm of a glad new year.

And what shall we find in the New Year Land?
Pleasures we sought that the old year
    banned?
The wealth and the leisure we've dreamed
    about?
All of the ills of the past shut out?

Is this what we seek in the New Year Land?
Or do we ask only to understand
The will of the Father, that we may do
Work in His kingdom the whole year through?

This shall we find in the New Year Land –
Just what we carry in heart and hand,
It all will depend upon you and me,
Whate'er we make it the year will be._

– Home and Foreign Fields
– Marian Phelps

New Year Thoughts

Let us walk softly, friend;
For strange paths lie before us, all untrod,
The new year, spotless from the hand of God,
Is thine and mine, O friend.

Let us walk straightly, friend;
Forget the crooked paths behind us now,
Press on with steadier purpose on our brow,
To better deeds, O friend!

Let us walk gladly, friend;
Perchance some greater good than we have known
Is waiting for us, or some fair hope flown
Shall yet return, O friend!

Let us walk humbly, friend;
Slight not the heart's east blooming round our feet;
The laurel blossoms are not half so sweet,
Or lightly gathered, friend.

Let us walk loving, friend;
We cannot tell how long this life shall last
How soon these precious years be over past;
Let love walk with us, friend.

Let us walk quickly, friend;
Work with our might while lasts our little stay,
And help some halting comrade on the way.

TEMPERANCE MATERIAL

Short Temperance Speech

I do not think it best
To wait till I'm a man,
But sign the temperance pledge
As early as I can.

Let's be teetotal boys
Till we grow up and then
'Tis my opinion, with God's help,
We'll be teetotal men!

The Human Engine

To be given after a brief description of how alcohol affects the normal functions.

You know the model of your car;
You know just what its powers are;
You treat it with a deal of care
Nor tax it more than it will bear.

But as to self,–that's different.
Your mechanism may be bent,
Your carburetor gone to grass,
Your engine just a rusty mass.

Your wheels may wobble and your cogs
Be handed over to the dogs,
But on your skip and skid and slide,
Without a thought of things inside.

What fools indeed we mortals are
To lavish care upon a car,
With ne'er a bit of time to see
About our own machinery!

– John Kendrick Bangs

Temperance

Don't send my boy where your girl can't go,
And say, "There's no danger for boys, you
    know,
Because they all have their wild oats to sow";
There is no more excuse for my boy to be low
Than your girls,
Then please don't tell him so.
Don't send my boy where your girl can't go,
For a boy, or a girl, sin is sin, you know,
And my baby boy's hands are as clean and
    white
And his heart as pure as your girl's tonight.

Salute To Youth!

You are the hope of the world;
You are radiant with energy;
You are undaunted by "impossibilities";
You believe in the basic honesty of men;
You face life as a great adventure;
You dream noble dreams;
Your marching feet beat a symphony of progress!
    Of you we expect great things;
    The conquest of disease;
    The outlawing of war;
    The dawn of the more abundant life;
    The harmonizing of industry;
    The creation of beauty;
    The revival of the spirit!
        As you march into the future with banners flying,
        Eyes shining with the splendor of your ideals,
        We doff our hats and stand at salute!
        For you are the hope of the world!

                                – Wilferd A. Patterson

The Jewel Case

(Adapted from "Scientific Temperance Instruction in Public Schools," in "The Frances E. Willard Contest Reciter" (No. 17) compiled by Anna A. Gordon.)

Take a full-jeweled watch. Put it in a case made of gold, then into one made of silver, and then into one made of porcelain. It will keep just as good time in the cheap case as in the costly one, because there is no interdependence between the watch and its environment.

God has wound up a "watch" in the snug round box on top of your head, warranted with good usage to tick right on for many years, – a watch with a mainspring of reason, the balance-wheel of judgment, the fine jewels of imagination and fancy, the dial plate of the human face divine, and the pointer of a character thereon.

This wonderful watch, the human brain, cannot keep as good time in a coarse case as in a fine one, for there is the closet interdependence between the brain and its environment, – between the tissues of the body and the tempers of the soul.

Brain, the wonderful thing in the body, controls the intricate machinery. Give clear thought and get clear action; give crazed thought, get crazed action. The physical law is sure. Alcoholic drinks have no place in a well ordered life.

Character is . . .

Bounded on the North by Sobriety
Bounded on the East by Integrity
Bounded on the West by Industry
Bounded on the South by Gentleness

SOBRIETY (habitual temperance; calmness seriousness)

The whole realm of invention, each day enlarging and constantly requiring better trained faculties, the clear eye, the steady hand, is putting such a premium on sobriety of life in all respects as will afford one of the surest and most far-reaching safeguards of a wholesome life that men can know.

INTEGRITY (uprightness; virtue; honesty; soundness; unimpaired or unbroken state of anything; purity; etc.)

In the book of Psalms, we read of David's being chosen by God to lead the nation of Israel. David had been faithful to his task when taking care of the sheep on his father's land, so God desired him for the larger task. In Psalm 78:72 we read:

"So he fed them according to the integrity of his heart; and guided them by the skillfulness of his hands."

INDUSTRY (Steady application to business or labor; productive labor; and industrial art, etc.)

The muscles are the "middlemen" between mind and matter. The industrious nerves are the message-bearers. Alcohol strikes the brain the moment it (alcohol) goes around the body. Almost immediately the switchboard is out of order. They move in unwieldy fashion. The hand cannot grasp things easily and the foot reports distance inaccurately. The main is transformed from a toiler to a reeler. Sobriety outranks industry.

GENTLENESS (softness of manners; mildness)

The perfect flower of strength, the ornament of industry, the fragrance of integrity, gentleness cannot live without sobriety. That is its vital breath, its native air. For gentleness is the "governor" of character's great engine, the plumb line of its perfectness, the binnacle that holds its compass true. So that when you have "boxed the compass," you shall find sobriety the virtue that dominates all others, since the clear, calm, normal brain turns the pointer of all human hope. Why should it not be so? This body that we live in is in a sense the universe to us. We get no light save that which comes in through this strange sky-light of the brain. The man wonderful lives in a house beautiful, and it is all in all to him.

In his ignorance man began to use strong drinks, and honestly call them a "good creature of God." But the attractive ingredient in all these beverages is alcohol, – a poison that has this changeless law, that it acts, in exact proportion to the quantity imbibed, upon the brain and nervous system, precisely as fire acts upon water, – lapping it up with a fierce and insatiable thirst. Alcoholic beverages are the only ones on earth that have no power of self-limitation. One glass says two, and two says three, until, as a general rule, from the power of self-perpetuation in this appetite, the life of a drinker of alcohol has but two periods.

In the first, he could leave off if he would, and in the second, he would leave off if he could.

How about the Round Box on the top of your Head? Are you protecting your "Watch-Case"?

A Modern Model

Two children were chattering together when one said to the other, "You're better lookin' than your daddy." "'Course I am," came quick response, "I'm a later model."

We may be later models than our fathers and mothers, and very much later models than the Pilgrim fathers and mothers, but after all, it isn't the outside that counts, it's the inside of our human machines that counts. It's the inside which determines what we are.

The first automobile manufactured did not have the gleaming chromium finish that the beautiful high-powered model of today has, but it had an engine. Paint and beauty in a car are of no value if the engine is left out, or if it is not in good working order.

The human body is a wonderful thing with its God-created parts, but, if we ruin that body, we cannot buy any spare parts. Let's be careful of our Twentieth Century "models." Let's take care of all the parts and keep them in good trim. Let's keep out the things that would ruin life. Science tells us that one thing the paint on the care needs is ethyl alcohol, but that one thing the human body DOES NOT NEED is ethyl alcohol, – in fact, it tells us that nothing harms the body more than ethyl alcohol.

Today we see new models for homes, for school buildings, for business buildings, for automobiles, for railroad trains, air planes and steamships. Over in England, in 1934, there was a very wonderful temperance exhibit. In one section of the exhibit was a model steamship in relief. By its side was a poster which read: Many Fine Ships Have Been Ruined By Alcohol.

CRAFTSMANSHIP **SPORTSMANSHIP**
FRIENDSHIP **CITIZENSHIP**

A CRAFTSMAN is a skilled artisan. Go and look up a craftsman in your home city. Watch him at work. Alcohol as a beverage would ruin his craftsmanship, for alcohol dulls brain centers and muscle action. Alcohol ruins craftsmanship.

A SPORTSMAN is one who pursues the sports. The athlete who wins in the game is usually the one who is a total abstainer from beverages of alcohol. A sportsman needs a strong body, a keen eye, a clear brain. Alcohol ruins sportsmanship.

FRIENDSHIP means good will toward one another. Through friendship we work together, play together, and build together. Alcohol has ruined many friendships. Those who believe in total abstinence from beverage alcohol do not want to be seen in the company of a friend who thinks he or she must drink because it seems to be popular, so the friendship is broken. Alcohol ruins friendship.

CITIZENSHIP is a blessed heritage, – enjoying rights in a state or nation! Good citizenship builds a nation, bad citizenship wrecks it. Alcohol as a beverage ruins citizenship for it robs a man of the best that is in him. Alcohol ruins citizenship.

– H.L.B.

Thanksgiving

T antalizing odors greet one everywhere;

H appiness is drifting through the chilly air;

A pples, nuts, and raisins – mince and pumpkin
    pie;

N ever such a turkey, all to satisfy;

K infolk all arriving, some from far away;

S uch a lot of laughter, Such a lovely day!

G rapes and cakes and cookies, jelly, sauce, and
    jams;

I n the piled up pantry, plates full of ham;

V egetables, chicken, plum pudding, sure
    enough!

I n the yard and hallway a game of Blind Man's
    Bluff;

N ot a soul but surely, on this thankful day,

G lad to greet Thanksgiving in a thankful way!

– L.D. Sterns

It Is Time To Give Thanks

Psalm 150:1

1. For the Son, who died for us.
2. For the Scriptures, which were written for us.
3. For Salvation, which was purchased for us.

– Harry G. Hamilton

On Thanking God

"I will mention the loving kindnesses of the Lord, and the praises of the Lord, according to all that the Lord hath bestowed on us" (Isaiah 63:1).

"Be content with such things as ye have" (Hebrews 13:5).

Begin by thanking Him for some little things, and then go on, day by day, adding to your subjects of praise; thus you will find their numbers grow wonderfully; and, in the same proportion, will your subjects of murmuring and complaining

97

diminish, until you see in everything some cause for thanks-giving. If you cannot begin with anything positive, begin with something negative. If your whole lot seems only filled with causes for discontent, at any rate there is some trial that has not been appointed you; and you may thank God for its being withheld from you. It is certain that the more you try to praise, the more you will see how your path and your lying down are beset with mercies, and that the God of love is ever watching to do you good.

– Priscilla Maurice, (The War Cry)

Thanksgiving

"Not unto us ascribe the praise,
But to our God our hearts we praise
In thankfulness, that He can bless
His people with His righteousness,
Use them to tell in every land
The saving power of His right hand!"

Thanks Be Unto God

(2 Corinthians 9:15)

1. The gift is beyond speech, "unspeakable" (1 Timothy 6:14, 16).
2. We employ melody to aid speech (Ephesians 5:19).
3. Below the melody is the heart overflowing (Psalm 103:1; Titus 2:14).
4. At the very best neither time nor eternity are sufficient to sing it all (1 Thessalonians 4:17; Hebrews 13:8).
5. As Saviour, cannot all be told (Acts 4:12; Ephesians 3:8).
6. As Lord, cannot tell it all (Ephesians 4:15).
7. As King, cannot tell it all (Isaiah 14:7; Revelations 19:16).

– Henry Ostrom

Thanksgiving

Once more the liberal year laughs out,
    O'er richer stores than gems or gold;
Once more with harvest song and shout
    Is nature's bloodless triumph told.

Our common mother rests and sings,
    Like Ruth among her garnered sheaves;
Her lap is full of goodly things,
    Her brow is bright with autumn leaves.

And we today, amidst our flowers
    And fruits, have come to own again
The blessings of the summer hours,
    The early and the latter rain.

To see again our Father's hand
    Reserve for us the plenteous horn
Of autumn, filled and running o'er
    With fruit, and flowers, and golden corn.

We shut our eyes, the flowers bloom on,
    We murmur, but the corn ears fill,
We choose the shadow, but the Sun
    That casts it shines behind us still.
Oh, favors every year made new!
    Oh, gifts with rain and sunshine sent!
The bounty overruns our due,
    The fullness shames our discontent.

                         – J.G. Whittier

Thanksgiving

My God! Thou art a God of strength and
    beauty!
Thou art the mighty Keeper of the seas;
Thou givest me my life, my faith, my seeing–
And I, so small – what can I give for these?
Thou givest me the sun, the hills, the rainfall,
Clear eyes to see the daybreak and the night,

A mind to fathom truth and follow straightly,
And I, so small, what can I give of might?

And then as though Thou countest not these
    blessings,
Thou sendest Thine own Son to die for me –
And I, so small – oh, humbly and with
    gladness,
I give my all – I give my life to Thee!

Thanksliving

It is fine to say we're thankful
    For all that we possess,
It is fine to put it plainly
    In words and not suppress
One item in the total score;
    But if our thanks be true –
We'll prove it, not so much in words,
    As by the deeds we do.
The act speaks louder than the word,
    And though our words be good –
The little deeds in kindness done
    Are better understood;
Thanksgiving may be given voice
    In tones which loudly ring;
But to show best true thankfulness –
    Thanksliving is the thing.

A Thanksgiving Prayer

(Recitation for a small child, who is holding a doll.)

I thank thee Father in the skies,
    For this dear home so warm and bright;
I thank thee for the sunny day,
    And for the sleepy, starry night.
I thank thee for the Father's arms,
    So big and strong, to hold me near;

I thank thee for my Mother's face;
    I thank thee for my dolly dear.
    (holding her doll out)
I thank thee for the little birds
    That eat my crumbs upon the sill;
I thank thee for the pretty snow
    That's coming down so soft and still.
O Father, up there in the skies,
    (looks upward)
Here me on this Thanksgiving Day,
    And please read in my little heart
The "thank yous" I forget to say.

A Thanking Prayer

Thank you, heavenly Father,
For the home I love so well,
For my father and my mother
And for more than I can tell –
For the food and clothes I wear,
For the dear friends everywhere,
For your love and for your care,
I thank you, heavenly Father.

Thanksgiving

For each little ray of sunshine,
For each tender blade of grass,
For the gently rolling meadows
Over which the shadows pass;

For the night-time and the moonlight,
And the stars that twinkle so,
For the music of the raindrops;
And the silence of the snow;
For the seed-time and the harvest,
For a place where I can pray,
And a heart of understanding –
I am thankful, Lord, today.

VALENTINE'S DAY

Valued Valentine

One heart somewhat lopsided,
Red color streaked a bit,
With lines or downhill printing,
And yet it makes a hit.
A slightly crooked arrow
Some lace stuck on awry.
And yet this precious token
Delights a mother's eye.

– Louise Darcy

My Valentine

I lost my heart to you today,
"Finders keepers" – or, so they say,
That's why I ask, my valentine,
Return YOUR heart instead of mine!

– Violet M. Roberts

February's Gifts

The gifts of February are –
Skies of warmer blue,
Days that are longer,
Suns that are stronger,
And a valentine for you.

Valentine Cousin
by Charlotte Middaugh Markell

"Mother, I have something to tell you," Janice cried, rushing into the kitchen when she came from school.

"And I have something to tell you, Janice," her mother laughed, "and I hope what you have to tell me is as nice as what I have to tell you."

"Well, I'm afraid is isn't," Janice said as she put her coat away in the closet. "But, let me tell first and have it over."

"Why, what can it be that makes my little girl so worried?"

"I'll tell you, Mother." Janice untied a parcel which she had brought home with her and laid a row of valentines on the kitchen table.

"Why, how pretty they are, dear," her mother looked at each one closely.

"Yes, there is one for Bess and one for Paul and two for the Hatch twins and one for the Ellis baby and one for my teacher."

"Well, they are all right."

"But don't you see, Mother? I haven't any for my valentine cousin, my cousin May, out West," Janice sobbed. "You know we always send each other valentines, though we have never seen each other."

"Yes, I know, dear," her mother answered, "but I gave you money for May's valentine, too."

"Yes, I know you did, Mother, and I got it, but here's what happened. You know that new girl in the grade above me, the girl named Daisy? Well, I heard some of the girls in her grade saying they were not going to put any valentines in the school box for her, because they hardly knew her."

"Yes, go on," Janice's mother urged.

"Well, I knew how I'd feel to be new in school and only get a few or no valentines at all. I put the one I had for May in the box in Daisy's room so she would be sure to get one nice one. It was the nicest one I had," Janice began sobbing again, "but now I haven't one to send May."

"I'm glad you were so thoughtful for the stranger," her mother said, "and now stop crying. I am quite sure May will not send you a valentine this year."

"Why, Mother, what do you mean?" Janice began. Then her eyes grew wide as she watched her mother open the pantry door, and out came a curly haired girl, just a little older than Janice. She was a little shy at first, then ran to put her arms about Janice. "Surprise!" she cried. "I am May, the valentine cousin."

"But how did you get her?" Janice asked, her eyes shining with pleasure.

"May came with your Aunt Carrie while you were at school dear," her mother answered. "That was what I had to tell you. Your Aunt Carrie said she decided it was about time that you two valentine cousins had a chance to get acquainted."

"Oh, how nice! Will you stay a long time, May? I'm sorry about the valentine. You did hear didn't you?"

"Yes," May laughed, "I couldn't help it, hiding to surprise you, but I am glad, for we decided to come so quickly, I had no chance to get a valentine for you."

"Oh, goody," Janice exclaimed. "Then tomorrow we can give each other a real live valentine – we can be valentines for each other."

A Valentine For Mother

A valentine for Mother dear,
As lacy as can be,
With hearts and cupids on it, too,
And sent, with love, from me.

For Mother is my valentine,
As true as true can be,
And so I sent the nicest one
To her, with love, from me.

For valentines are just for those
That we love best, you see,
And so I send the nicest one
To her, with love, from me.

Making Valentines

I'll take a bit of paper lace,
And little heart or two
And make a pretty valentine
Especially for you.

– Harvey Peake

A Valentine For Daddy

A valentine for Daddy dear,
To say I love you true,
To say I know you work for me
The whole day through.
To say I know I could make light
Your heart, if I would do
As many pleasant, thoughtful things
As you do for me, too.
A valentine to Daddy dear,
To say I'll try my best –
Because I love you, Daddy,
Of all valentines, the best!

A Friendship Valentine

Somebody cares for you,
Cares so much,
That the heart grows glad
At your slightest touch;
And the sound of your voice
And the sight of your smile
Make all my burdens
And cares worthwhile.
Somebody cares for you
Bye and bye,
When years roll on,
You will know it's I;
Then, looking back –
O'er the road we've fared,
You'll see how much for you
Somebody cared!
A friend is one who takes your hand
And talks a speech you understand;
Who's partly kindness, partly mirth,
And faith unfaltering in your worth;
Who's first to cheer you on success,

And last to leave you in distress;
A friend is constant, honest, true –
In short, a friend is "Just Like You."

WELCOMES AND RESPONSES

Welcome

I come to bid you welcome,
At this glad time of the year.
This is a day of rejoicing
And our hearts are filled with cheer.
I come to bid you welcome,
Thrice welcome, one and all,
It's grand to have you here tonight,
In answer to our annual call.

Welcome

I say welcome to you all, – right welcome to our hall, our hearts, and to hear what we have to say. I tell you, you are just as welcome as you can be. We are real glad you are here. We wondered if you would come, we wanted you to come, we are glad you have come, we thank you for coming. Now, you know you are welcome. What could we do without you? You always encourage us, and if we make mistakes, say, never mind, try it again. We love our friends. We see them here. They know we have been making ready, and that we shall try to do our best. Mine is a speech of welcome. It is a first-rate one, but it means just what it says.

Welcome

"How beautiful upon the mountain are the feet of them who bring us good tidings." We feel that you are here to bring a great message and to render a great service in the sight of the Lord today. We therefore welcome you with all joy and hospitality to our midst. We thank God for your devotion to His cause and your love for humanity. You are evangelists because you carry the good tidings of Jesus to those who know him not. You are ministers because you seek to minister to those who need the Lord in their daily activities and contacts, and in His name you are ever ready to encourage the living, bless the dying, and comfort those who mourn.

This church stands with open doors to welcome all mankind who, like you, appear among us in the name of Jesus. May your meeting today be filled with the Holy Spirit and it is our prayer that we may gladly fulfill any request made of us if we are called upon to render service in your behalf, whether it be great or small. To those of you who come from far away we open our homes that you may rest therein and our hearts that you may find fellowship there. To those of you who we have met for many years at this same place for this same cause, we extend our cordial welcome as well, in as much as old friends are the best of all. Those who have never attended this meeting before we ask your cooperation and extend to you the hospitality of the house of God, above which there is no higher, no greater hospitality. To you all we say – welcome! Twice welcome! Thrice welcome!

Welcome

Kind friends and patrons here today,
We're glad to see you all,
We'll try this kindness to repay,
Although we know we're small.

We're small and yet we feel quite big,
But don't expect too much;
Some people judge folks by their rig,
But we don't care for such.

We're here to have a jolly time,
And help our school along,
And those who cannot make a rhyme
Will have to sing a song.

Don't be too prim, and don't be rough
Just have a pleasant meeting;
But I have spoken long enough
To give you all a greeting.

WELCOME FROM THE USHER BOARD
OF THE _____ CHURCH

To our pastor, fellow church members, guests and friends of the _____ Church, we extend the heartiest welcome that can be given by one body of Christians to another. We thank you for your presence here today to worship with us in the installation of our Usher Board, (or give other purpose here). We appreciate the fact that out of busy lives you have graciously come under our roof to share in a service which marks the consecration of a band of Christ's followers. We pray that you may find true fellowship here with us today because we are Christians who honor and follow the same Lord and Master, Jesus Christ. Our service will be a simple one but we sincerely and fervently hope that you will derive some message and benefit from it.

"It isn't the thing that we get, dear friends,
And it isn't how much we know;
It's the will to serve, it's the hand we lend,
It's the light which our lanterns throw."

That is the idea for our service for today, that we may reflect the light of the One who lived so long ago and yet still lives in our hearts. He called us the Light of the World, and again He called himself the Light of the World. We are to be the true reflectors of the great Light and in His name today we are consecrating a group of Christian workers to the further service of His church, the Bride of Christ. May you catch a vision of the Light, and no matter how flickering the flame may be, may you hold it high, and as you leave our hospitable walls may you be filled with deep spiritual satisfaction which causes you to say within your own heart, "it has been good to be here."

Response To Welcome

Master of Ceremonies, Honored Guests, Members and Friends:

The sage writer of Proverbs wrote many centuries ago: "Words fitly spoken are like pictures of gold in a network of silver." This verse comes to my mind as I reflect on the warm words of welcome which have fallen, like golden music, upon our ears this afternoon. Surely Mrs. _____ has painted a picture of gold and placed it in a network of silvery words, as she so cordially welcomed us to this house of God, which makes me very humble as I attempt to respond to this address of hospitality. We appreciate the friendly smiles and the warm words of welcome which have been given us in this hallowed place today, and, if we have had burdens, they are lifted; if we have had sorrows, they are scattered: if we have had problems they are solved. Solomon said, "Heaviness in the heart of many maketh it stoop, but a good word makes it glad." We thank you for those "good words" today, which have lightened our hearts and made them glad.

We are grateful not only for your presence here, but for the spirit and attitude of appreciation which caused this program to be prepared today. We thank you for your interest, for your prayers upon her behalf and mine, for your continual show of friendship and concern for our welfare. But we thank you all who have come to do her honor today at this testimonial service and it is our prayer that we both may be impelled to serve better, and inspired to witness more sincerely and reverently to the saving power of our Lord and Saviour, Jesus Christ, because of this day, because of this service, and because of your thoughtfulness and Christian love. Thank you very much.

Welcome To Strangers In Your Church

To the crowds that throng the city streets,
    Or jostle in the marts of trade;
To carefree youth whose joyous feet
    Dance through the world that Thou has
    made,
To masters in the realm of thought;
    And toilers all, beneath the rod;
To lonely hearts by men forgot,
    Be this to each – The House of God.

WOMEN'S WORK

A Million Women

– Mary Beth Fulton

"Women own 50% of all our industries; Hold 65% of the wealth of the world; Are the beneficiaries in 80% of all life insurance policies; Spend 85% of the family income."

A recent estimate gives the total number of Baptists in the Northern Baptist Convention as a million and a half. If it is true that two-thirds of our congregations are composed of women, what is the part of 'a million women' in the kingdom enterprise?

The first missionary was a woman. "Go and tell . . ." were the words said to Mary at the sepulcher by the angel. And the message of the resurrection that she took to the disciples that day has been carried into the uttermost parts of the earth.

What of the messengers – those faithful ambassadors for Christ? There are about fifteen hundred women in our denomination who because of age and infirmity are no longer able to "hold aloft the banner marked for love and peace." Their average age is 72 – many are in the eighties and some in the nineties.

Will 'a million women' hold them in their prayers and remembrance? In their hunger we should provide nourishment; in their weakness, strength; in their loneliness, fellowship.

"One woman – can be forceful.
One hundred women – can be helpful.
Once thousand women – can be powerful.
One million women – united – are invincible."

MARY McLEOD BETHUNE

"Get wisdom, get understanding: forget it not." Proverbs 4:5.

Sometimes it is a lot of fun to be a member of a great big family – and then sometimes it's not so much fun. Mary McLeod enjoyed it. There were sixteen other children in the family. With their mother and father they lived in a three-room log cabin on a rice and cotton farm about three miles from Mayesville, South Carolina. While Mary was still quite young she exhibited distinct traits of character and was truly a ray of sunshine in the home. Full of enthusiasm and ambition she was happy to have the privilege of going to school, although she had to walk five miles and back. Mary determined then that when she grew up she would make it possible for others boys and girls to gain that pearl of great price – education.

Mary McLeod was a bright, apt scholar and deeply interested in her studies. She was the recipient of two scholarships and had no difficulty in completing her training at the Moody Bible Institute in Chicago, Illinois, where she was the only Negro student at that time. Because of her quick understanding and sweet and sympathetic nature her classmates loved her and did their best to keep her happy.

During her two years of teaching in Sumter, South Carolina, she met and married Albert Bethune, a fellow teacher. After the marriage they moved to Savannah, Georgia, where they spent two years of quiet life. During this two-year period their only son, Albert McLeod Bethune, was born.

Her greatest ambition was to serve the race, and so she began her career at a mission school in Palatka, Florida. This work was truly an incentive to her, for during the ensuing years, she proved a blessing to Negro youth. She was the founder of the Daytona Normal and Industrial Institute. Her early struggle in maintaining this institution was heartbreaking, but her indomitable will bore her through those discouraging years. Her burning zeal and enthusiastic spirit so fired the interest of others that she won for her school loyal supporters.

In July, 1923, the Daytona Normal and Industrial Institute came under the notice of the Board of Education of the Methodist Episcopal Church, and was merged with

Cookman Institute, thereby becoming co-educational. It was then known as the Bethune-Cookman College. This college offers many various phases of instruction, which gives the students opportunity for development and growth.

May Mary McLeod Bethune's life of noble service be such an inspiration to Negro girls and boys that they will strive to make of their own lives monuments of achievement.

My Obligation and Duty to My Church

– a Woman

I have accepted Christ into my life, and because He was willing to save a poor sinner like me, I owe my Saviour the best that is in me. My talents are His to use; I owe Him my service and devotion, my all. I must be willing to be used and, when opportunity presents itself, to render unto others what Christ would have me to do. I must be willing to learn, that I might be better able to serve in His great cause that the work of the church and the spreading of the "good news" may reach unto all nations.

I must not only be willing to serve, but in serving to witness for my Christ and to tell others of the marvelous love and redemption found in Christ Jesus. Along with this, I must not forget that as I live, so am I. My actions will speak as loudly as anything I may say.

I owe it to my church to desire to grow in grace and the consummation of that desire through a life of prayer and Bible study, that my service be unto His glory and not due to my own strength. Through my own spiritual growth and that of others in the church the spiritual strength of the church itself is measured.

I must attend its services of worship, prayer, study, and the observance of its ordinances as far as within me is possible. And I must interest others in church attendance, that through my contacts with them and their attendance the unsaved who thus come may be won to a saving knowledge of Christ Jesus.

I owe the church my financial support. As the Lord has prospered me, so must I give, that through the combined giving of all believers the Lord's work may go on. I believe strongly in tithing. I must help support missions by giving of my money, and if I am not called to go to the "uttermost parts of the earth," it behooves me to support those whom the Lord does send. Or, if it be the needy who need my help, God help me to render them what aid I am able.

I owe my church the qualities of a great character, a virtuous life, a sense of dependability, a right attitude of kindliness and love toward my neighbors and all with whom I come in contact, to be just in my dealings with all my fellow men, to help in time of need, sickness, or distress, to be temperate in all things, to avoid intoxicating liquors or anything harmful to the body, and to be true to my own country by following the precepts as necessary to good citizenship.

Above all, I must not forget to remember my fellow men in prayer, and strive that, through all things, those who are lost may be won to a saving knowledge of what Christ has done for them through His death and resurrection. He died that we might be saved. I must share this experience with others.

There are many more obligations and duties which I owe my church that I could name, but let me end with this: When I remove from the section where I have my church membership, I owe it to my church and to my Christ to move my letter to a church of like faith in my new field of habits or endeavor.

I fall far short of my duties and obligations to my church, but God's grace is sufficient to help me in my stumbling ways if I but turn to Him who is my Guide and Helper.

– Salt Lake City, Utah

Grandmother's Spectacles

"My grandma's spectacles are queer
    It's almost like a game;
She says she has two pairs of them,
    Although they look the same.
One pair makes tiny things seem big,
    "Enlarged," she says it's called;
The other makes big things seem small
    I s'pose they are ensmalled.
I saved some choc'lates for her once
    Some teeny little ones
She said I was "an angel" an'
    They looked "as big as buns!"
But when I dropped my mug, and made
    A big spot on the mat,
She said, "It won't be seen at all,
    A little thing like that!"
I'm saving all my pennies
    And I' going to buy two pairs
Of spectacles for others
    The kind my grandma wears.

Your Place

Somewhere the world has a place for you
    That is all your own;
Somewhere is work that your hands can do,
    And yours alone.
Whether far over land and sea
    Or close at your door may the duty be,
It calls for your service full and free
    Take your place!

Somewhere the world has bitter tears
    Your smile might dry;

Somewhere the burden of doubts and fears,
  The hopeless sigh.

There are steps that falter, weary, weak,
  For the strong, brave arm they vainly seek.

Will you pass them by on the journey bleak?

  Take your place!

Somewhere the world has a desert spot
  Your toil might till:

Somewhere a life whose loveless lot
  Your love might fill.

If the place that waits be high or low
  Question not, care not – onward go!

The world's great battle needs every blow
  Take your place!

– Blanche Trennor Heath

Thoughtlessness

They say the world is round, and yet
  I often think it square,
So many little hurts we get
  From corners here and there;
But one sad truth in life I've found,
  While journeying east and west,
The only folks we really wound
  Are those we love the best.
We flatter those we scarsely know,
  We please the fleeting guest,
And deal full many a thoughtless blow
  To those who loves us best.

When You Know Him

When you get to know a fellow, know his
    every mood and whim,
You begin to find the texture of the splendid
    side of him,
You begin to understand him, and you cease
    to scoff and sneer,
For with understanding always prejudices dis-
    appear.
You begin to find his virtues and his faults you
    cease to tell,
For you seldom hate a fellow when you know
    him very well.

I Would Like To

I am not bound to make the world go right,
    Nor even to improve my neighbor's yard
    (But I would like to)
I cannot shut his hens up day and night;
    And this, I will admit, is rather hard
    (For I would like to)
I cannot silence noisy passersby,
    Who, late at night, awake me with their song
    (But I would like to)
I cannot understand why good men die,
    And bad men live to work their deeds of wrong
    (But I would like to)
I will not let my criticisms roam,
    But make my garden bloom as the rose
    (And this I can do)
With wire fences keep my chickens home
    And walk consistently with friends and foes
    (And this I will do)

The power of example may be felt,
    And quietness and order may increase
    (All this we hope for)
The chicken yards may form a safety belt,
    And bring a neighborhood of lasting peace
    (All this we pray for)

Perhaps

If you can drive a car when all about you
    The homeward rush is on at five o'clock
And know you're right when all the family doubt you,
    And red lights flag you down at every block;
If you can trust your instinct to inform you
    Which way the man in front intends to turn,
Though he hasn't given any sign to warn you
    Excepting that his stoplight starts to burn;
If you're content to drive the speed that's safest,
    Regardless of the speed by law allowed,
And, knowing you are good, can still give credit
    To those who are with greater skill endowed;
If you can use your horn and not abuse it
    When those in front are creeping like a snail
The boulevard is yours to have and use it,
    And, what is me, you may keep out of jail!

If One Has Failed

If one has failed to reach
    The end he sought,
If out of effort,
    no great good is wrought,
It is not failure, if the object be
The betterment of man;
For all that he had done
    and suffered is but gain
To those who follow
    seeking to attain
The end he sought.

117

His efforts they will find
   are guidepost on the way
To that accomplishment which he,
   for some wise purpose,
      could not be the factor in.
There is a need of unsuccessful effort;
'Tis the need who mission
   is to lie beneath
The soil that grows the laurel wreath,
   and he is not unworthy
Who falls struggling manfully
   to do what must be done,
      in dire distress,
That others may obtain success.

— William J. Lampton

Give Me The Man

Give me the man with the heart to fight,
When they deem him down, if his cause is right,
   The man with the wit and the will to sing
   And to breast the storm with a broken wing.
Give me the man with the heart of a child,
Who trusts with a faith that is undefiled,
   The man with the tenderness, goodness and grace
   That glorifies woman, to shine in his face.
Give me the man with the eyes of the seer,
The zeal of the prophet, the pride of the peer,
   The plod of the peasant, a clown and king,
   The mosaic man, made of most everything.
Give me the man with the dew of the dawn,
The glow of the twilight when sunlight is gone,
   The flush of the Spring, the calm at the close
   Of the dear dying year with its storms and it's snows.
The warmth of the Summer, the Autumn's cool breath,
The rapture of life and the wonder of death,
   Give me the man that is cosmos and clod,
   A brother to me and a brother to God.

Little Things Make Great Ones

One step and then another,
　　And the longest walk is ended;
One stitch and then another,
　　And the largest rend is mended,
One brick upon another,
　　And the highest wall is made;
One flake upon another,
　　And the deepest snow is laid.

A little theft, a small deceit,
　　Too often leads to more;
'Tis hard at first, but tempts the feet,
　　As through an open door.
Just as the broadest river run
　　From small and distant springs,
The greatest crimes that man has done
　　Have grown from little things.

A Little Boy's Speech

They thought I couldn't make a speech,
　　I'm such a little tot!
　　I'll show them whether I can do
　　A thing or two, or not.
Don't be afraid to fight the wrong,
　　Or stand up for the right,
And when you've nothing else to say,
　　Be sure you say – Good night.

New Neighbors

It's always so exciting
　　When people move to town,
We have new next door neighbors,
　　Bob says their name is Brown.
They have a boy named Jimmy,
　　And such a pretty girl;
I heard her mother call her,

So her name must be Pearl.
Bob says the boy is jolly,
   He helped him find his ball
As soon as they are settled,
   I think I'll go and call.

– Daisy M. Moore

The Starry Dipper

The Dipper hangs in the midnight sky,
   All twinkly with stars of gold.
It's a puzzle to me just what it can be
   This sparkling Dipper may hold!

Sometimes it's tipped up, and sometimes down,
   And I cannot help wondering why
Nothing ever is spilled to the ground
   From the Dipper that hangs in the sky!

– Daisy M. Moore

A Little Boy's First Recitation

I think it's not an easy task
To speak a piece in school,
But still I do not wish to ask
To be excused the rule.

For little boys must some day take
The places of the men,
And if they would good speakers make,
Must try and try again.
This be our motto; and now here
I'll close my little rhyme,
Hoping, should I again appear,
To better do next time.

Little Chatterbox

They call me "Little Chatterbox,"
    My name is Little May
I have to talk so much, because
    I have so much to say.
I love my papa and mamma,
    I love my sisters too,
And if you're very, very good
    I guess that I'll love you.
I think it is so nice to live,
    And yet, if I should die,
The Lord would send his angel down
    And take me to the sky.

The Golden Wedding

Fifty precious golden links
    In cupid's blessed thrall,
Who shackles victims two by two
    Enslaved beyond recall.
Fifty years of golden sun,
    With just a dash of tears,
Intermingling in the flood
    Of all those golden years.
Fifty years of traveling
    Together hand in hard,
Wandering down life's lovers' lane
    That leads to Sunset Land.
Fifty years of happiness,
    Fifty years of love;
Just another matchless match
    Made in heaven above.

February Birthdays

The twelfth of February,
    I am sure you all must know
Is quite a famous birthday
    Of a boy of long ago.
And I am very happy
    That my birthday comes that day.
Each year I have a party,
    With flags and music, gay.
And when I read of Lincoln,
    And his deeds so fine and true
I want to grow up like him,
    And serve my country, too.

                – Winifred Catherine Marshall

Patriotism

It means "love of one's country,"
I looked it up you see,
A man who's patriotic,
Is what I mean to be.
I want to serve my country;
And keep my ideals high,
Like Washington and Lincoln,
Whose deeds will never die.

                – Winifred Catherine Marshall

INSTALLATION FOR CHURCH AND SUNDAY SCHOOL OFFICERS AND TEACHERS

(Suggestions for Using the Installation Service)

The officers and teachers of the Sunday School should be formally inducted into their offices each year. This service should include every one who is to be in a position of leadership in the school.

The installation service may be used most appropriately at the beginning of the Sunday school year, this being the first Sunday in October.

The installation of officers and teachers comes properly at the regular preaching hour, preferably in the morning, or at whatever hour the work of the Sunday school may be most effectively magnified.

The pastor's sermon for the occasion should be brief and in harmony with the spirit of the consecration service. The following subjects may be suggestive: "Apt To Teach"; "The Responsibility of Teaching Religion"; "The Church and the Home Working Together"; "Jesus, the Master Teacher."

Ample preparation should be made for the service. Each officer and teacher should be thoroughly informed as to the contents of the program and should know in advance what the covenant contains. Any worker unwilling to take this covenant should be allowed quietly to withdraw from official relationship to the school.

The workers in the church school should sit together near the front of the church. Some simple decorations, consisting of ferns and flowers, will be appropriate. Following the service, opportunity may be given for the parents to meet the officers and teachers.

Remember, this is a consecration service. For that reason it should be made an occasion of real worship for the ones being installed and for those otherwise participating. It should be an occasion of real dedication on the part of the workers to God and to the Church and challenge them with the greatness of their task.

INSTALLATION SERVICE

Organ Voluntary.
Processional Hymn: "Lead On, O King Eternal"
The Apostles' Creed (repeated in unison).
Prayer by the Pastor
Solo: "This Is My Task"
Scripture Lesson: Deuteronomy 6:4-9 (or 1 Timothy
    4:6-16)
Read by the superintendent
Announcements and Offering
Hymn: "O Master, Let Me Walk With Thee"
Sermon

At the close of the sermon the pastor may say: We are at the beginning of another Sunday school year, filled with opportunity, responsibility, and service. Shall we make it a year of real achievement in the building of Christian lives? To realize such a task and to express our true appreciation of the great challenge it presents to us as a church, we come to this service this morning motivated and dominated by the spirit of consecration. Our powers, our desires, our plans, our hopes, and all that we are, we would consecrate to Jesus Christ, our great Teacher.

(Let the chairman of the Board of Deacons or the Sunday School Superintendent come forward.)

Pastor: The Sunday School Superintendent is responsible for the supervision of all Christian education in the local church, including within its scope all the children, young people, and adults. This places a tremendous responsibility on this office. As Superintendent it will be your privilege and opportunity to lead all Sunday school officers into an effective discharge of their duties and to challenge them to do the work which they are supposed to do. Will you faithfully promise by the help of God to prepare yourself for this responsible position and will you endeavor to lead your co-workers to a growing appreciation of their task?

Superintendent: I will endeavor so to do with the help of God.

(Let the superintendents of all the Sunday school departments come forward.)

Pastor: You are called upon to organize and administer the work of your departments intelligently and efficiently. It is a part of your responsibility to advice with and encourage your teachers and helpers; through precepts and example guide the members of our school into the fullness of Christian character. Do you assume these responsibilities and will you endeavor to execute them faithfully?

Answer: I assume these responsibilities and will endeavor both to prepare myself for them and to execute them faithfully.

(Let all secretaries and treasurers come forward.)

Pastor (to the secretaries and treasurers): The records and reports of the work of our Sunday school are of great importance both for the present and future. It will be your duty to keep in constant touch with every department of the school; to know the status and achievement of all the officers, teachers, and pupils; to have this data in such shape that it may be available at a moment's notice. Will you exercise due diligence in preparing, using, and preserving these records?

Answer (in unison): I will consecrate my talents and time to this office, and will endeavor to be faithful in performing these duties.

(Let all teachers, department and class officers come forward and stand in a semi-circle around the officers.)

Pastor (to the teachers and other workers): You will come into intimate and vital contact with the pupils of this school, and your influence upon their lives may be most potent. Will you faithfully and diligently study your Bibles and such helps as your Church makes available? Will you try to lead your group in genuine experience of Christian fellowship during the coming year, and to win the lost to Christ?

Answer (in unison) (to all): I will endeavor so to do by the help of God.

Pastor: It is a matter of great importance that all officers and teachers be regular and punctual in attendance. May we depend upon you to meet the requirements faithfully?

Answer (in unison): You may depend upon us.

Pastor: A call to service is also a call to preparation for efficient service. Our Church makes special provision for the training of its workers. Are you willing, as you have opportunity, to pursue such courses of study as are available, and thereby endeavor to equip yourself further for this great work?

Pastor: In this great work of guiding Christian growth, example counts for much. Will you as officers and teachers, endeavor to practice the Christian virtues of faith, love, patience, honesty, diligence, and loyalty?

Answer (in unison): I will.

Pastor: This is a school of Christian Education by which the church is seeking to lead children, youth, and adults to follow the Christian way of life. Will you strive earnestly to walk more perfectly in this way, and seek to lead those under your care to know and follow Jesus?

Answer (in unison): I will endeavor to do so by the help of God.

Pastoral Petition: O Father, seal these mutual vows of thy servants, our officers and teachers, as an abiding and an availing covenant with thee and this church. Amen.

(Let the congregation stand).

Pastor (to congregation): Brethren, you have heard these workers take upon themselves very solemn obligations. You will realize that these duties which are theirs are voluntarily accepted on behalf of all for whom we are responsible in this community. You are aware that their word cannot be successfully done without;the co-operation of the home and the community, that you as parents and citizens be willing to perform your part of this task faithfully. Will you therefore cooperate with these workers by encouraging enlistment of new members, and regular and punctual attendance of your children?

Answer (in unison): We recognize our responsibility and will cooperate to the best of our ability.

(Let the congregation be seated.)

Let the officers and teachers repeat in unison the following:

Worker's Covenant

In consideration of my election or appointment to a position in the Sunday school, I promise, by the help of God, to do my best to live up to the following provisions during the coming year:

1. To live a sincere and consecrated Christian life.
2. To recognize as one of my primary responsibilities helping those with whom I work to develop into Christlike personalities.
3. To attend preaching services as regularly as possible and to cooperate with the total program of the local church.
4. To be present and on time every Sunday unless providentially hindered.
5. To prepare myself thoroughly each week for the responsibilities and duties which I have to perform.
6. To maintain vital week day contacts with the pupils, such as visitation, committee work, study, outings, personal conferences.
7. To attend regularly the meetings of the Worker's Conference and of my department council, unless prevented by some valid reason.
8. To increase my own efficiency and to make possible high standards of work through special reading and study, taking at least one training course this year, or reading at least one approved book in church school work.

9. To remember that I am a member of a group or team of Christian worker, and that I must bear my share of responsibility and must also recognize that others have important duties and responsibilities.

Silent prayer (all workers kneeling):

Singing of hymn by a quartet or choir (softly):

"Lord, Speak To Me That I May Speak."

Benediction, with workers still on their knees. If preferred, the pledge below may be used instead of the "Worker's Covenant."

A Pledge For Officers and Teachers

I solemnly pledge myself before God and in the presence of my fellow-workers to pass my life in purity and to practice Christianity faithfully. I will abstain from whatever is harmful and mischievous and do all I can to transform myself and those I teach and with whom I work into genuine children of God. I will do all in my power to maintain and elevate the standards of teaching Christ and will hold as precious each soul committed to my keeping, and will share all inspiration and experience that comes to my knowledge in the practice of my calling. With loyalty will I endeavor to aid the pastor and leaders in their work and devote myself to the upbuilding of the Kingdom of God.